Neurosphere

Neurosphere

The Convergence of Evolution, Group Mind, and the Internet

Donald P. Dulchinos

WEISERBOOKS
Boston, MA/York Beach, ME

First published in 2005 by
Red Wheel/Weiser, LLC
York Beach, ME
With offices at:
368 Congress Street
Boston, MA 02210
www.redwheelweiser.com

Library of Congress Cataloging-in-Publication
Dulchinos, Donald P.
  Neurosphere : the convergence of evolution, group mind, and the Internet /
Donald P. Dulchinos.
     p. cm.
  Includes bibliographical references.
  ISBN 1-57863-349-4
  1. Electronic villages (Computer networks) 2. Cyberspace. 3. Convergence
(Telecommunication) 4. Computers and civilization. I. Title.
  TK5105.83.D83 2005
  303.48'34—dc22

                         2005026346

Typeset in Janson by Anne Carter
Printed in the United States
VG

12 11 10 09 08 07 06 05
8 7 6 5 4 3 2 1

The paper used in this publication meets the minimum requirements of the
American National Standard for Information Sciences—Permanence of Paper for
Printed Library Materials z39.48-1992 (R1997).

To Effie Dulchinos
For everything, and for that magical library on the wall of the breezeway
that nourished my interest in books.

To Ted Dulchinos
For everything, and for recommending Man's Unconquerable Mind.

Contents

Acknowledgments

Thanks to Steve Solomon, Marji Cooney Solomon et cetera, Carl (then) DeMatteo, and Gerry Coleman, who were there for the seminal extemporaneous homo electric discussions.

Thanks to Stuart Booth, who believed in the manuscript through the vagaries of publishing mergers and acquisitions. Also for the simpatico editing job.

Thanks to Jack Emery Taylor of Jetpax for the logo and the literary companionship.

And thanks to Carolyn, Zoe, and Teddy for putting up with the interminable tap-tapping.

Introduction

"Sing to the ancient harmony!"

—FROM "NIGHT'S SWEET DAUGHTER" BY THE MYSTICS (WORDS AND MUSIC BY JOHN STEVENS)

THE INTERNET, as I write, is an unprecedented phenomenon occurring at the end of an accelerated century. It is so profound in its transformation of economic behavior that it causes people to view it as millennial—truly the end of an era. It is the beginning of something so new that we have only vague ideas about its ultimate scale and scope. Even the bursting of the dot-com bubble has not really changed anyone's opinion of its long-term potential.

As if the commercial hype were not enough, the economic impact of the Internet pales beside the effect it is going to have on our social and personal lives as it becomes ubiquitous. The Internet will transform many of the essential things that make us human—communication, cooperation, thinking, and most of all, our search for meaning.

Moreover journalists, paying great attention to millenial religious movements as one century melts into the early years of another, are helping to make these changes more apparent. Although concepts of advent, of the second coming of the Christian Messiah, have been a part of our Western culture for centuries, their revival has had a profound impact on American society (evangelical Christians) and the world (Islamic fundamentalists). The real force in play, however, is the convergence of the phenomenon of the Internet with the urgent spiritual seeking that has grown as material well-being has brought social and individual stability. This book is very much about the religious impact of the Internet.

I know the word "religion" carries all sorts of baggage—baggage dictated by the religion to which you either subscribe or have rejected. When I speak of religion, I speak not of any particular sect or any culture's interpretation of its encounter with the divine. I refer rather to the common ground of humanity's search for meaning, its hunger for a glimpse of humanity's future development, and the feeling that, despite all our surface differences, we are somehow all part of one entity—call it what you will.

This book begins with the story of my personal experience of unity in something I call a group mind—an experience mediated by the Internet. That experience provided me with visceral proof of the theory I put forward in the rest of this book—that a mind, a connected human experience, is arising from the physical brain and central nervous system called the Internet. The Jesuit paleontologist (*not* an oxymoron) Pierre Teilhard de Chardin saw this coming in the days between the two World Wars. He called it a *noosphere*, which I have updated to the more pronounceable *neurosphere*. In Teilhard's view, the telegraph, the telephone, and, later, television, were all part of the very evolution of the species. We will take a summary view of Teilhard's theories and put forward many more visions of wholeness that have arisen persistently over human history in fields as diverse as literature, physics, and psychology.

The Internet itself represents technology catching up with Teilhard's vision. It is the most obvious instance of the evolution of an infrastructure for the neurosphere. I have spent more than a dozen years on and around the Internet and the industries that have built this infrastructure. My experiences seem, in retrospect, just part of the inexorable process of networked technology developing into something that is not just *like* an organism, but is apparently alive.

This is not hyperbole or exaggeration. In fact, telecommunication and information technologies are increasingly integrating themselves into the human body itself. Electronic prosthetics, direct neural implants, and the brain's control of electronic and mechanical limbs are moving the boundary that used to exist between man and machine to some undefined frontier inside our bodies and our brains, and perhaps inside our minds. And if the electronics inside my brain connect directly with the electronics inside your brain, how is it meaningful to speak as though we are not part of one larger entity?

4

Virtual Communities

"In Harmony, great efforts will be made to bring together the devotees of extremely rare manias. For each of them the meeting will be a pilgrimage as sacred as the journey to Mecca is for Moslems."

—CHARLES FOURIER

WHEN LOOKING FOR signs of global change, it's always best to begin locally, within your own community. My community, these days, is not so much the town in which I live, but a shared virtual space on the Internet called the Well. How did this come to be?

The phenomenon of computer-mediated communication began years ago with ARPAnet, later called the Internet. This computer network was invented by the U.S. Defense Department's brightest minds to preserve telecommunication capabilities in the event of a catastrophic nuclear war. Although the network was created for that purpose, however, its spare capacity was quickly adopted by scientists who wanted to share their research, and then their hobbies.

As the civilian world became aware of the potential of data-communication technology, businesses began to exploit this potential by creating electronic "spaces" where individuals could meet and talk. The mega-corporation now called AOL Time Warner started from this humble premise, and a number of scattered virtual communities slowly grew around this and several other online services. Among the communities drawn to this new medium were a bunch of ex-hippies led by Stewart Brand, editor of the *Last Whole Earth Catalog*. Born of an experiment by Brand and the staff of *Whole Earth Review* (the magazine spawned by the *Last Whole Earth Catalog*), the Well was an online computer service dedicated exclusively to discussion of various topics—no graphics, no video games, no sports scores, just conversations spread out over time. The Well participants' slogan was simple: "What it is is up to us."

GETTING IN THE WELL

I was a subscriber to the Well long before the advent of the World Wide Web. I found great enjoyment in this activity, joining in conversations on topics important to me that I couldn't share with my everyday friends and acquaintances—comparative religion and psychology on the intellectual side, basketball on the mundane side, and telecommunication and computer technology for my professional interests. Indeed, it was the latter that really justified in my mind the $15–$20 a month I spent in those pre-Internet days to dip into the Well.

When my wife and I moved to Boulder, Colorado in the spring of 1994, we looked for a discussion area—or "conference" in Well parlance—that talked about life in Colorado and the Rocky Mountain region in general. After several months of settling in, new-job angst, and some exploration, a group of Colorado residents (including myself) and other Well subscribers with interests in the Rocky Mountains started a new conference on the Well called Rockies. The Rockies shared an interest in the romance of the cowboys and Indians and exchanged information and opinions on various regional topics and outdoor activities such as skiing.

We were all pleased and a little surprised at how quickly a little community developed. One thing group members had in common right from the beginning, besides a willingness to use a new technology, was a great deal of satisfaction with and pride in the quality of life available to them in Colorado. As a new arrival, I was especially vocal, as only the recently converted can be. I should add that my wife never did and never has joined the Well. She met some Well people when we lived in Washington who fit the "computer nerd" stereotype a little too well (and had bad table manners), and she decided that she just wasn't interested.

In fact, in its early years, computer conferencing, even about nontechnical topics, was dominated by men because it took a determined technical professional to master the technology. The Well was unique in its somewhat larger minority of women, but even there, women felt compelled to carve out a private, women-only space to preserve the dynamics of feminine interaction.

The Rockies group started to attract new participants from different parts of the country with family ties to the region or to outdoors interests. What startled many of us was how we began to discover different links between individuals. As personalities established themselves in the group, people inevitably started talking about things they had in common in their personal lives. A death in the family of one was a cause for mourning for all.

People often tell me they don't understand how I can form a personal relationship with someone I've never really met. This is, in many ways, the fundamental premise of this book. In the virtual world of the Well, we actually meet at a level that is, in many ways, more essential to who we are than the small talk that often passes for friendship in the "real" world. Because all subscribers pay for their time online, they tend to focus more clearly on what is really important to them. But another element of the Well serves to cement these relationships in a broader way—F2Fs, or face-to-face meetings.

F2Fs became popular in the San Francisco Bay area where many original Well members lived (and still do live). Originally centered around activities like monthly gatherings at Chinese restaurants or outings to baseball games, these activities served to bring people together in the flesh. Not surprisingly, some of these online friendships turned into intimate relationships and even marriages.

Computer-mediated communication has a unique characteristic that gives it a unique value. It allows individuals to communicate, yet remain unknown, at least in some respects. This can be good or bad. Several Well participants are wheelchair-bound or otherwise so disabled that getting around town is hard work for them. The Well and forums like it give them a meaningful way to get "out." Others who have a hard time in social situations because they are, or believe themselves to be, unattractive physically, or because they are not verbally agile and are perceived, at best, as quiet or, at worst, as dull and boring, have found some protection in virtual space. Virtual spaces level the playing field, if you will, so these individuals can participate in ways they might otherwise find difficult.

On the Well, people get to know each other by posting the thoughts and feelings most important to them. And some, ultimately, form relationships. Despite the "bad rep" that the Internet has acquired as a place of anonymous "cyber sex" (which amounts to little more than phone sex transposed to a different medium), it has also been the starting place of many significant relationships.

I watched one adulterous relationship develop in our group. Rather than take offense, however, the group sided with the woman leaving her husband, celebrating the new couple as one of their own. The husband tried to stalk his wayward wife online, but eventually gave up. In the "real world," we might see this as just a little bit tawdry and even unbalanced. As I watched this online dynamic, however, I was struck by the notion that the electronic connections that had been formed were more powerful, and somehow deeper, than ordinary friendships. The woman, after all, opted for her virtual partner over her husband.

A NEW KIND OF COMMUNITY

Ever since computers were called electronic "brains," it was inevitable that people would start to theorize about their effects on the nature of humanity. Howard Rheingold, a technology writer and early Well enthusiast, wrote a book called *Tools for Thought*, a phrase taken from J.C.R. Licklider, a researcher and professor at MIT. Licklider was among the first to see computers as more than efficient number-crunching automatons and analyze them as devices that could help individuals think and perform more efficiently. In Rheingold's view, the computer could also serve as a more effective tool of communication than any experienced so far. Rheingold went on to write a book called *Virtual Communities*, whose point of departure was his experience on, not so coincidentally, the Well.

I have struggled to define how the community Rheingold foretold has become part of my thoughts, not just on a conscious, but on a subconscious, level. The closest I have come to articulating this is to call my friends on the Well "a community that lives in the back of my mind." Their comings and goings and achievements and disappointments are tracked over time just as other people track their families and close friends. In some ways, because of the everyday nature of the medium, this community has become even closer to me than my "real world" communities. I'm part of it, as it is part of me.

The communal characteristics of the Well first became apparent to me while living in Washington, D.C. The first few meetings of Well habitués that I experienced were characterized by the immediate development of deep conversations that so swiftly bypassed small talk that it amazed me, living as I did in a city where small talk is a prerequisite of day-to-day political life. It was here that I observed an eye-opening incident. I watched as a certain cross section of the Well that had begun to leverage their online experiences to further their careers as journalists, lawyers, and financial analysts specializing in the Internet phenomena were galvanized into concerted action.

Not long after the World Wide Web opened the Internet to the average, nontechnical user, we started to hear the first horror stories of people being swindled and kids being exposed to pornography on the Internet. Predictably, the Internet was exploited early on by frauds and sexual predators—as had every other advance in communication before it. Journalists, lawyers, and analysts who opposed such exploitation came together online and combined their talents to debunk a *Time Magazine* horror story. It is not the result of this collaboration that interests me, however. It is the clear and early demonstration of a "group mind" that came together to investigate the subject. It was a very informal process, and a very organic one, made possible by the community of interest that already existed within the physical infrastructure of the Well.

Rheingold documents many examples of this phenomenon in *Virtual Communities*—examples that point to how the Internet and related online technologies encourage the formation of community. It is important to emphasize, moreover, that the idea of "community" as defined in these examples is real community.

Some Well users question the notion that these online communities are "real." Their arguments are valid in some instances, and certainly these communities have characteristics that distinguish them from communities defined in other contexts. In one case, however, the user's actions seem to have contradicted his arguments, since he was consistently among the most prolific posters and ubiquitous presences on the Well. When diagnosed with terminal cancer, he even went so far as to hold his own online wake. He was unrepentant of his stand on the issue of community until the end, but in this case, the medium was indeed the message.

The ease with which communities and group minds are formed in virtual spaces is also illustrated by the negative characteristics of those groups. This was described by a friend who participates in Echo, a New York-based forum similar in structure to (though different in personality from) the Well. While referring to yet a third such entity, a Union College alumni group called Virtual Schenectady (or VS, after the city where the college is located), this individual reported:

> On the Echo BBS we have a regular mob phenomenon we call "The Next Big Thing," whereby collective boredom or angst builds into a big ball of acrimony which is vented like the blowhole of a baleen whale. Just like on Echo, VS seems to enjoy the same phenomenon, which occurs in regular cycles. And given that such a routine doesn't seem to exist in the offline world, I must conclude that it's peculiar to this medium.

Given these examples, it is also not surprising that online technology and behavior ultimately intersected with another collective pursuit—politics.

ELECTRONIC DEMOCRACY

Political activists of all stripes are eager to adopt new ways to make their influence felt. Online communication networks offer some real opportunities to reverse the increasing distance citizens feel from their government. The pace of modern life seems to increase inexorably, and as people make trade-offs, they choose to spend time as soccer moms rather than as political activists or even interested voters. The benefits to special interests, with paid advocates watching the political process closely and cultivating close relationships with elected officials, increase in equal and opposite measure to the disengagement of a majority of citizens. But what if technology could level that playing field?

A new phenomenon in the computer networking world emerged with the appearance of Cleveland Free Net—a nonprofit organization formed to give more people more equitable access to email and other online technologies. Other so-called "community networks" arose that aggregated information about different geographical communities, usually no larger than a single metropolitan area. These networks ranged from government information services, to community calendars, to other types of resources. This type of information service was familiar to many by this time through cable television access channels, with their scrolling local announcements. That format was almost impossible to use, however, because it was not indexed and could not be searched for specific information. The concept was good, but the technology was limited and could only support one-way communication. Nonetheless, the information was out there, albeit in various incompatible data formats. And even a bloated bureaucracy was either unable or unwilling to support the creation of easy two-way access for all.

Indeed, easy access to searchable data was still a new concept to 80 percent of the population in the U.S. as late as 2000. Things change slowly, and some changes lose momentum. But the opportunity remained, and soon products like Microsoft's Sidewalk, CitySearch, DiveIn, and AOL's Digital City appeared, marketed by major telecommunication corporations seeking to capture the "community network" market. These sites, unfortunately, have developed largely into newspaper listings translated to the Internet and generally exist only as vehicles to sell advertising. They make almost no attempt to foster discussion areas, and thus provide little more than lip service to the idea of community.

By contrast, as a member of the Board of Directors of the Boulder Community Network, I was committed to helping BCN develop into a force for electronic democracy that could change the way we look at ourselves as citizens and Americans. I was committed to the principle that the closeness allowed by the technology could truly recapture the idyllic democracy of early America's town meetings. And I'm not talking here simply about the use of online polls. I'm talking about a true electronic democracy based on conversations that go on for days or weeks, with time for reflection on complex policy issues. These online exchanges get us a lot farther than one-hour televised town meetings once every couple of years. Real democracy is grounded in the exchange of ideas and the participation of a truly representative body of citizens. Voting just ratifies the decisions that are made through debate and collaboration. Through electronic democracy, we can resurrect the body politic, a group that acts as a single organism.

THE INTERNET AS TEMPORARY AUTONOMOUS ZONE

In a democracy, where majority rules, minorities are frequently disenfranchised. Pornographers were among the first minority to identify the potential of the Internet to distribute their particular narrow brand of content. However, a number of other equally small (and much less offensive) minorities discovered the Internet comparatively early in its career. They view the Internet as a tool to preserve minority thought—however unpopular or even heretical. This intellectual diversity is essential to a healthy world society.

Author Hakim Bey (*aka* Peter Lamborn Wilson) wrote an essay in 1986 called *Temporary Autonomous Zones* (TAZ). Bey saw the Reagan years as the final death knell for organized resistance to the concentrations of economic and political power achieved in the 1960s. The Reagan revolution drove the outcasts and heretics who had flourished in the Sixties from their place in American society, forcing them to find temporary havens to engage in their countercultural activities.

Many of these like-minded souls discovered that the Interne
virtual spaces where they could voice their rebellious thoughts
erwise impossible communities. *Temporary Autonomous Zones* ma
pervasive piece of writing on the Internet to this day. Author/edit
ance artist R. U. Sirius, whose *Mondo 2000* magazine was a seminal vehicle
for cyberpunk thought, once wrote:

> We've built ourselves a virtual country, a permanent TAZ, those of us who
> have faced the American clampdown. Our Subterrani exists, a supranational
> nation. Anyone who wants to join can find a way in. Government agents and
> counterintelligence people can get in as easily—but what will they gain com-
> pared to what they may lose? There's no organization to bust in here. There
> are no leaders—everyone's a leader. There's a net of minds only loosely con-
> nected to identities, physical OR virtual. Breaking up the American under-
> ground is like trying to bust the planetary Net . . . they tried that, and they
> failed. And the government infiltrators, what danger they're in! Immersed in
> the siblinghood of an entirely imaginary underground, many of them will
> listen and understand . . . and slip their leashes and join the struggle for real,
> because an anarchist counterforce that checks and balances the central gov-
> ernment is as American as apple Macturnovers.[1]

Following is a short list of some of these subcultures with a presence on the
Internet:

African Americans

Native Americans

Zapatistas

Survivalists

Libertarians

Religious drug users

Recreational drug users

Homosexuals

S&M practitioners

Neoprimitives

Artists in general

Science fiction subculture

New Age practitioners, health and spiritual

Cohousing developers

Independent (small budget) film fans

This observation by David Cox, of the Royal Melbourne Institute of Technology in Australia, could apply as well to the community found on the Internet:

> I've taken my inspiration from regions in most cities which can be best described as bohemias: the most interesting parts of town. Usually these places are vibrant points of exchange between groups and individuals. They are places where freedom of expression is highly valued and where diversity and tolerance reign supreme.[2]

It is this and some other dimensions of the burgeoning Internet that lead me to see the World Wide Web as a phenomenon that brings people together more intensely than television or even telephones.

From Darwin,
to Teilhard,
to McLuhan—and Back

"In Pére Teilhard's view, the increase of human numbers combined with the improvement of human communications has
fused all the parts of the noosphere together, has increased
the tension within it, and has caused it to become "infolded"
upon itself, and therefore more highly organized. Mankind as
a whole will accordingly achieve more intense, more complex,
and more integrated mental activity, which can guide the
human species up the path of progress to higher levels of
hominization."

—JULIAN HUXLEY

MARSHALL MCLUHAN coined the phrase "global village" to describe the effects of universally available broadcast television, a medium that allows people to share, in close-to-real time, the experiences of other people who are geographically and culturally distant. His metaphor was quickly strained by the one-way nature of the communication. My family, like many Americans, had starving Biafrans in our living room in the 1960s, but very few Biafrans had Americans in their lives. My mom imploring me to finish my supper because Biafrans were hungry had little or no impact.

Perhaps my lack of response was due to the callousness of childhood, but I think it was rooted in a major drawback of the medium itself—the lack of dynamic communication between geographic regions. Nevertheless, global television was a dramatic step toward a greater awareness of the diversity of cultures; and it generated at least some incrementally greater level of understanding between some of those cultures.

The Internet, considered as a communication medium, serves to extend McLuhan's metaphor, not only into something more like a real village, but into a village that communicates on a deeper level than many real villages. My experiences on the Well have confirmed this for me by demonstrating sharp contrasts between the closeness I experience in my virtual relationships and the distance I remember feeling in the small town where I grew up—a real place where I felt few real connections and where I maintain few long-term friendships.

Prior to joining the Well, I have been fortunate to share other group friendships, including a fraternal literary society that sometimes sought group action. In the fervor of youth, we sometimes felt an invisible group mind take hold and drive our actions toward common goals without the need of explicit verbal communication. A 19th-century member of the same group described it this way: "In that closest circle of earthly fellowship, wherein I have known what it is for heart to be knit with heart."[1]

The power of communal movements, as well as the madness of crowds and mob rule, have been recognized for years. However, the first individual to propose that the entire population of human individuals might constitute the beginnings of a single thinking entity was neither a computer scientist nor a sociologist specializing in technology. He was a Jesuit trained as a paleontologist named Pierre Teilhard de Chardin.

TEILHARD–FATHER OF THE NOOSPHERE

Born in Clermont-Ferrand in the Augverne region of France, Pierre Teilhard de Chardin took his first vows in the Society of Jesus in 1902. Teilhard studied paleontology beginning in 1912 at the Paris Museum of Natural History. His parallel interests converged during World War I. In the winter of 1916, during a lull in the activities of his regiment in Belgium, Teilhard's philosophical view began to emerge: "Over the landscape of loss and disintegration that stretched out on every side," biographers Mary and Ellen Lukas tell us, "he superimposed his vision of another world—healthy whole and growing."[2]

> I think one could show that the front isn't simply the firing line. . . . When you look at it during the night, lit up by flares, after a day of more than usual activity, you seem to feel that you're at the final boundary between what has already been achieved and what is struggling to emerge.[3]

Teilhard's study of the evidence for evolution led him to attempt a reconciliation of the eschatology of Christianity with the facility of evolution. This was not a synthesis in which the Catholic Church took any particular interest. *Le Phénomène Humain* was completed in 1941, but Church authorities refused him permission to publish for almost fifteen years. In fact, the book was published posthumously in 1955 and translated into English as *The Phenomenon of Man* in 1959.[4] The book laid out Teilhard's view, as summed up by biologist Julian Huxley, that "man was evolution becoming conscious of itself."[5]

The Convergence of Species

As a paleontologist, Teilhard speculated in the context of his understanding of evolution, which was informed by his religious belief in life having purpose and direction. (This is a synthesis that seems to be beyond the contemporary advocates on either side of the evolution/creationist divide.)

For Teilhard, the differentiation of nervous-system tissue stands out as a significant transformation in the history of life on Earth. "It provides a direction; and therefore it proves that evolution has a direction."[6] At another level of differentiation, he observed, humans developed brains just as tigers specialized in claws.

In Teilhard's view, the key characteristic of the evolutionary process that led to humans is one of convergence. He observed that the higher you go up the evolutionary chain, the smaller the variety among the members of a species. The phenomenon first appears in the emergence of mammals. Then *homo sapiens* emerged as a single branch of the primates and ceased further physical evolution as it has successfully inhabited every ecological niche. With the emergence of humanity, he claims, evolution has "overtly overflowed anatomical modalities."[7]

Teilhard then posited that convergence reoccurs on the societal level in the form of the "late capitalist world consumer unit."

> With social convergence comes traditions and collective memory. This is the beginning of the group mind of humanity, the *noosphere*. What are the intricacies of our social forms if not an effort to isolate what are one day to become the structural laws of the noosphere?[8]

The Evolution of Consciousness

Teilhard viewed consciousness as a product of evolution. (More recently, biologist Francisco Varela defined this as the "emergent" view.) "As molecules become more complex, they also gain more of an interior component which is the forerunner of what we call consciousness." (Physicist Nick Herbert agrees; see chapter 4.) In a cell, Teilhard points out, "what we have is really the stuff of the universe reappearing once again with all its characteristics—only this time it has reached a higher rung of complexity and thus, by the same stroke . . . advanced still further in interiority, i.e. in consciousness."[9]

Stephen Jay Gould and others argue that there is no "progress" in evolution, but this view willfully ignores the existence of God and dispenses with any meaning or purpose at all in the universe. It is an extremist position in the sciences.

Teilhard's romantic view, on the other hand, based in careful observation and reflection, would certainly infuriate the likes of Gould. "If there were no real internal propensity to unite," wrote Teilhard, "even at a prodigiously rudimentary level—indeed in the molecule itself—it would be physically impossible for love to appear higher up, in hominised form."[10]

As human evolution ceased in the biological realm, Teilhard proposed that evolution in the brain was channeled into the human "ability of consciousness to take possession of itself as of an object."[11] In more poetic and yet more precise terms, the evolution of consciousness is characterized by "the elaboration of ever more perfect eyes within a cosmos in which there is always something more to be seen." Even more precisely, humanity is "evolution become conscious of itself."[12]

From there, the evolution of consciousness, in the absence of a physical medium in which to act, has manifested itself in humanity's social evolution. Teilhard's claim anticipates biologist Richard Dawkins' neologism, the *meme*.

Freed of biological constraints, Teilhard saw human activity increasing in speed and in intensity of communication. He also observed the great speed of evolution of human consciousness illustrated by the characteristic artifacts of each age. The appearance of species ranging from Neanderthal to modern *homo sapiens* happened in virtually the same geologic era, unlike the evolution of dinosaurs who only changed over several long geologic ages. In a relatively short period of time, humans went from Neanderthals performing burial rituals to Cro-Magnon creating cave paintings, reflecting, in Teilhard's view, an evolution in consciousness.

In the context of this book, Teilhard's observation of the speed of consciousness evolution is reflected in the unprecedented technological and social phenomenon of the World Wide Web. Indeed, I believe the Internet represents the latest manifestation, in the material world, of the ongoing evolution of consciousness.

The Convergence of Consciousness

Humankind has spread into every corner of the planet without breaking up into species, so that we now form a "single membrane" over the Earth. This new layer, the "thinking layer," has spread over and above the world of plants and animals. In other words, Teilhard suggests that, outside of and above the biosphere, there is the *noosphere*.[13] The frame of our existence, according to him, is as follows:

barysphere

lithosphere

hydrosphere

atmosphere

biosphere

noosphere

Philosopher J.B.S. Haldane made the same connection, stating succinctly:

> If cooperation of some thousands of millions of cells in our brain can produce our consciousness, the idea becomes vastly more plausible that the cooperation of humanity or some sections of it, may determine what Comte calls a Great Being.[14]

The Technology of the Noosphere

Twentieth-century telecommunication technology, in Teilhard's view, is a mechanism for the inexorable evolution of this noosphere." And if humanity is an organism, then "we should endeavour to equip it with sense organs, effector organs and a central nervous system."[15]

Writing in the 1940s, Teilhard was already impressed by the rapid growth of technology. From the temporal perspective of a paleontologist, the industrial era certainly exploded on the scene almost instantaneously. From the data, Teilhard theorized that "the first new form of life appears suddenly in great numbers, as if from a supersaturated solution," and then ramifies and changes quickly. This is why the fossil record rarely shows "missing links." This speculation anticipates Stephen Jay Gould's more recent and formalized theory of "punctuated equilibrium."[16] Gould's theory is that evolution of new species takes place rapidly at the edges of ecological niches. The speed of the evolution and the rapid dominance of the new species means transitional mutants are rare in the fossil record.

If the industrial era and the information age are epochs of incredibly compressed growth and change, then surely the phenomenal adoption of the Internet by the general public and the corporate world after the introduction of the World Wide Web was an even more vivid confirmation of Teilhard's theories. The increasing integration of the Internet into people's lives—for shopping, for learning, for communication—illustrates the fullest expression of Teilhard's predictions. Each human, as Teilhard observed fifty years ago, "now demands not only food but a daily ration of iron, copper, electricity, cinema and international news."[17]

Teilhard predicted not only a unification of human consciousness, but that this would be a good thing. He was a good Jesuit; he believed that God loved humanity and that Jesus would return. He chose to treat Christian eschatology as a metaphor, and sought to fit the scriptures to the world as he saw it. For him, the ultimate unification of humanity was the Omega Point. In Christian terms, this was the equivalent of the Second Coming.

What I find most appealing is Teilhard's synthesis of science and faith, as reasoned from a base of scientific observation and an acknowledgment that existence has meaning. I think the world is still waiting for an answer to the death of God. Many people still attend church, but the myths and stories are no longer comforting. People are there, not because churches have answers, but because churchgoers still have questions. The anomie of modern life seems to result from an inability to find a reason to seek progress in the world—something that gives this material process a purpose.

Mob Rule and the Madness of Crowds

You don't need to be Christian to embrace Teilhard's observations and predictions, any more than you need to be a Satanist to challenge his Utopian vision. Teilhard certainly attempted to address criticisms. The obvious critique in the wake of Hitler's rise and fall was that anthill behavior or mob rule was as likely to result from unity as from fascism. Teilhard countered, "monstrous as it is, is not modern totalitarianism really the distortion of something magnificent, and thus quite near the truth?"[18] We may very well be on the verge of a consistent and simultaneous human experience. We may well be approaching the ability to act with a single will. Hitler, among others, exploited this. Consider, on the other hand, that perhaps apparently benign "personalities" Madonna and Barney the Dinosaur likewise wield a perverse influence on large populations, acting at some subconscious or preconscious level to create unity, even on this banal level.

Fear is a driver well understood by the mass media as something that galvanizes large populations. Demagogues have always had the ability to instigate witchhunts based on little or no evidence by literally demonizing some subset of the population. Demons are a ubiquitous archetype in the world's cultures and an easy way to drive mob action. Peter Russell, author of *The Global Brain*, carries this thought a step further, sounding this warning:

> Will this growing global brain turn out to be sane or insane? If civilization continues with its current self-centered, materialistic worldview, it will almost certainly bring its own destruction.[19]

Teilhard certainly did not believe that mob rule would flow inevitably from the formation of the noosphere. He foresaw that the primary characteristic of the noosphere would be sympathy.

This concept of all-pervasive sympathy is what defeats his critics. Teilhard admits that much wrong action takes place as a result of ignorance. But very few people do evil, he argues, if they have direct knowledge of the inner goodwill of others. If information—timely, accurate, and verifiable information—is available, it becomes more difficult for demagogues to drive action based on ignorance and fear. We are not insane when it comes to environmental degradation. We just haven't been convinced that the negative consequences out there are connected to our own actions. (Denial is, of course, another strong motivator, but usually can't be maintained when reality intrudes.)

Another popular critique of collective consciousness is that somehow it implies the obliteration of individual thought and action. "The only place where something like a global brain has reached popular culture is in the science-fiction TV series *Star Trek: The Next Generation*," one commentator claims. "In their version of the collective intelligence, the Borg, are about the worst enemies of human race, whose only aim is to 'assimilate' all remaining individual beings and thus destroy their individuality."[20] But this can only occur if you surrender your individuality.

In fact, most of the views of the future global mind do not presume the disappearance of the individual. Teilhard himself expected to see "each particular consciousness remaining conscious of itself at the end of the operation. Each particular consciousness becoming still more itself and thus more clearly distinct for others the closer it gets to them in Omega." [21] As writer Jim Starlin put it more recently, "Collective memory, collective heart; this atmosphere breeds understanding and mutes the ego."[22] Once we understand each other more fully, we are less likely to consign individuals to faceless stereotypes.

Collective thought and action do not entail acting with one will, but rather taking advantage of a faster and wider distribution of information—information about societal concerns and the causes of current politico/economic problems. Deeper, better-quality information can disseminate the story of each individual and societal segment to the group as a whole for analysis and action. Then, the world nervous system can act as a tool for those solutions (e.g., more efficient feedback indicators of environmental degradation). Maybe.

Teilhard further believed equity was inevitable in the noosphere. "[T]he entry into the superhuman [is] not thrown open to a few of the privileged nor to one chosen people. . . . They will open only to an advance of all together."[23] This may be, but observers have already noted that the Internet to date is the province of higher-income portions of the population. I believe, on the other hand, that, just as telephones—especially personal and mobile cell phones—have become nearly ubiquitous in the United States, Japan, and Europe (and increasingly so in the Third World), so will Internet access become a commodity available to all (see chapter 3). Whether all choose to take advantage of the technology and participate in some form of group consciousness remains to be seen.

Thus, the end of the world as we know it is, almost by definition, the logical outcome of Teilhard's thought. Consciousness is not an epiphenomenon or by-product of the physical body or brain; it exists above and beyond them. This leads to some interesting speculation, which we will revisit in chapter 4.

In summary, human evolution is convergent for Teilhard. We are the first or only species that has stopped branching into other species. We may have come to the end of physical evolution, but we've evolved as a species with the creation of a world-encompassing membrane of consciousness (electromagnetic and otherwise) and collective memory. In short, we've gone from the biosphere to the neurosphere. Teilhard's theory was a *tour de force* of creative thought. Moreover, it is confirmed by fifty years of ensuing scientific and scholarly activity, and perhaps some enhanced insight as well.

THE EVOLUTION OF CONSCIOUSNESS

In evaluating the notion of consciousness as evolutionary, it may be useful to address first the nature of consciousness itself. Teilhard's theories rest on a series of hypotheses:

> Consciousness evolves.
>
> Consciousness is not strictly an epiphenomenon of a single brain.
>
> Consciousnesses can combine and function as a single entity.

Teilhard was in good company, however, when positing the unity or wholeness of humanity. Moreover, his evolutionary approach is compelling in ways that other models of wholeness, such as Jung's theory of the collective unconscious, are not. A brief survey of other models of a collective consciousness illustrates that a number of thinkers have arrived at the same notion from different perspectives.

The Birth of the Mind

Princeton psychologist Julian Jaynes proposes that mind as we conceive it, distinct from a collection of instincts and Pavlovian behaviors, is a relatively recent phenomenon. In *The Origin of Consciousness in the Breakdown of the Bicameral Mind*, Jaynes proposed that, prior to between 10,000 and 5,000 BC, humans had no intuitive inner voice. Rather, they externalized that voice, a phenomenon described in Biblical and mythological literature as gods (or dead kings) talking to humans. As local situations changed, this inner voice became further refined and finally evolved into awareness of self and an ability for general abstraction.

The underlying physiological explanation for this is not that brain structure changed over a short period of time. Rather, the human brain had evolved up to that point to be enormously capable of adaptation to rapidly changing climates, such as the onset of the Ice Age. Proof of the brain's adaptability is common. For example, people who suffer damage to sectors of the brain associated with certain functions often have those functions taken over by different portions of the brain through new connections in existing tissue. Further, "it would be wrong to think that whatever the neurology of consciousness now may be, it is set for all time. . . . [It is clear that] the function of brain tissue is not inevitable, and that perhaps different organizations, given different developmental programs, may be possible."[24]

Is the development of telecommunication and its apotheosis in the Internet the type of rapid environmental change that brings about additional evolutionary changes in consciousness?

Consciousness as Emergence

The problem of consciousness is a vexing one to specialists in neurological medicine. A materialist position developed in the middle of the 20th century that the mind is nothing but the physico-chemical workings of the brain.[25] The first step away from that view was an agreement that purely subjective phenomena cause changes in brain activity. Under this model, "consciousness becomes an integral working component in brain function, an autonomous phenomenon in its own right."[26]

A group of researchers has come together in recent years to explore the implications of the existence of subjective influences further. They have conducted a series of conferences titled "Toward a Science of Consciousness" in an attempt to define consciousness in an operational sense.[27] David Chalmers of the University of Arizona, a leader of this group, has characterized what are now called the "easy" and "hard" problems of consciousness. The so-called "easy" problems include:

The ability to discriminate, categorize, and react to environmental stimuli

The integration of information by a cognitive system

The reportability of mental states

The ability of a system to access its own internal states

The focus of attention

The deliberate control of behavior

The difference between wakefulness and sleep

Chalmers explains at length:

> The really hard problem of consciousness is the problem of experience. When we think and perceive, there is a whir of information-processing, but there is also a subjective aspect. As Nagel (1974) has put it, there is something it is like to be a conscious organism. This subjective aspect is experience. When we see, for example, we experience visual sensations: the felt quality of redness, the experience of dark and light, the quality of depth in a visual field. Other experiences go along with perception in different modalities: the sound of a clarinet, the smell of mothballs. . . . What unites all of these states is that there is something it is like to be in them. All of them are states of experience.
>
> I suggest that a theory of consciousness should take experience as being fundamental. We know that a theory of consciousness requires the addition of something fundamental to our ontology, as everything in physical theory is compatible with the absence of consciousness. We might add some entirely new nonphysical feature, from which experience can be derived, but it is hard to see what such a feature would be like. More likely, we will take experience itself as a fundamental feature of the world, alongside mass, charge, and space-time. If we take experience as fundamental, then we can go about the business of constructing a theory of experience.
>
> In particular, a nonreductive theory of experience will specify basic principles telling us how experience depends on physical features of the world. These psychophysical principles will not interfere with physical laws, as it seems that physical laws already form a closed system. Rather, they will be a supplement to a physical theory. A physical theory gives a theory of physical processes, and a psychophysical theory tells us how those processes give rise to experience. We know that experience depends on physical processes, but we also know that this dependence cannot be derived from physical laws alone. The new basic principles postulated by a nonreductive theory give us the extra ingredient that we need to build an explanatory bridge.[28]

Chalmers' colleagues include members of the transpersonal school of consciousness, who agree that experience will be explainable by physical theory. But, unlike Chalmers, the transpersonal psychologists believe that physical theory itself must be expanded to take account of consciousness. They see consciousness as clearly transcending the boundaries of the individual brain.[29]

One typical transpersonal psychologist is Charles Tart, whose theory of emergent interactionism posits consciousness as an emerging system that is the product of two qualitatively different systems—the brain on the one hand, and the "mind/life" system on the other. This mind/life system exists independent of and prior to the development of consciousness by the human species. This is a little more radical, but a view that has its adherents dating at least back to Henri Bergson. The implications of this view will be explored at length in chapter 4. Tart believes that some so-called psychic, paranormal, or psi phenomena are the result of interaction between these two systems and proposes to investigate these phenomena as case studies. Thus, in contrast to philosophical theories of mind/body dualism, emergent interactionism has consequences that can be tested. For the purposes of this chapter, Tart's theory represents another suggestion that a new kind of consciousness may be developing or evolving now.

The sense that consciousness may be independent from an underlying biological organism finds some support in the work of Dr. John Lilly.[30] Lilly's experiments with sensory deprivation tanks appeared to demonstrate that mind, or at least the subjective experience of consciousness, could be moved around the body and ultimately leave it. The movie *Altered States* was a sensationalized version of Lilly's work. Not much in the way of experimental replication has occurred since then. However, this may be due simply to the somewhat controversial and vaguely disreputable nature of such work among neurological scientists.

The Nature of Evolution

Teilhard's spirit of increasing unity does not contradict Darwin, though it may appear to at first glance. While it is axiomatic that evolution is about the "survival of the fittest," the phrase does not imply that species evolve exclusively through competition. Biologist Lynn Margulis, for instance, has proposed a sort of biography of living systems. Prokaryotic cells (cells without nuclei) evolved, she claims, into eukaryotes (cells with nuclei) through the mechanism of an invasion by bacteria. These bacteria took up residence inside their sluggish hosts and became faster swimmers, carrying large numbers of genes and evolving in cooperation. Nature may not be fundamentally cooperative rather than competitive, Margulis notes, but it happens.

Several contemporary evolutionary theorists have presented formal theories that support other elements of Teilhard's proposals.[31] Richard Dawkins, in his book *The Extended Phenotype*, argues that social groups and the built environment do not just behave *as if* they are evolutionary, but are actually the embodiment and characteristic features of genes. Similarly, Stephen Jay Gould sees long periods without change, followed by times of rapid evolution of species. He calls this "punctuated equilibrium." If the industrial revolution and the information revolution are examples of extended phenotypes, then they are also representative of punctuated equilibrium (assuming some equilibrium will attain and be sustained in the aftermath of Web frenzy). I believe this leaves Teilhard's musings in rough congruence with a few of the ideas of leading contemporary evolutionary theorists.

In an interesting convergence of research from diverse fields, Danny Hillis, a supercomputer pioneer, built computer programs to mimic evolution. In so doing, he corroborated Gould. Hillis found that, in these programs, long periods of little or no change were followed by major change over a short time period. This is one of the key findings of contemporary chaos theory as well, providing a key for explaining many complex phenomena.

On another front, biologist Francisco Varela agrees with Teilhard that biological cognition is an emergent phenomenon. He says: "[My] sense of self exists because it gives me an interface with the world . . . [but] it can't be localized anywhere. It's distributed in the underlying network."[32] Christopher Langston agrees: "[There's] something in the dynamics of parallel, distributed, highly nonlinear systems which lies at the roots of intelligence and consciousness." Hillis responds (as if on cue): "[M]aybe it's telecommunications merging us into a global organism."[33]

Group Minds in Nature

Bees, ants, and termites all exhibit intelligence as an entire colony or hive, but not as individuals. Lewis Thomas, a physician and former director of the Sloan Kettering Institute, writes of termites:

> As more join in, they seem to reach a critical mass, a quorum, and the thinking begins. They place pellets atop pellets, then throw up columns and beautiful curving symmetrical arches, and the crystalline architecture of vaulted chambers is created. It is not known how they communicate with each other, how the chains of termites building one column know when to turn toward the crew on the adjacent column, or how, when the time comes, they manage the flawless joining of the arches.[34]

Nevertheless, Thomas observes that the idea of a group mind is not appealing when it is applied, as Teilhard did, to humans:

> What makes us most uncomfortable is that [ants], and the bees and termites and social wasps, seem to live two kinds of lives: they are individuals . . . and at the same time component parts, cellular elements, in the huge, writhing, ruminating organism of the Hill, the nest, the hive. . . . We do not like the notion that there can be collective societies with capacity to behave like organisms.[35]

Thomas, on the other hand, is perfectly comfortable with the notion.

> Although we are by all odds the most social of all social animals—more interdependent, more attached to each other, more inseparable in our behavior than bees—we don't often feel our conjoined intelligence. Perhaps, however, we are linked in circuits for the storage, processing and retrieval of information, since this appears to be the most basic and universal of all human enterprises. We have access to all the information of the biosphere, arriving as elementary units in the stream of solar photons. When we have learned how these are rearranged against randomness, to make say springtails, quantum mechanics, and the late quartets, we may have a clearer notion how to proceed. The circuitry seems to be there, even if the current is not always on.[36]

It is also interesting to note that one observation made by Thomas that predates the World Wide Web certainly finds confirmation in it:

> We spend our time sending messages to each other, talking and trying to listen at the same time, exchanging information. This seems to be our most urgent biological function; it is what we do with our lives.[37]

Likewise, bacteria have been discovered that produce a small molecule that diffuses readily through the cell wall in either direction. An increase in the population density of bacteria causes the concentration of this molecule to increase. A high concentration of this quorum-sensing molecule activates specialized machinery in the bacteria that is useless to the individual microbe, but quite valuable to a community of billions of microbes all operating similar machinery.

This quorum-sensing, cooperative activity was first noticed in marine animals that harbor colonies of phosphorescent bacteria. By keeping its light-producing machinery turned off when microbe density is too low for it to make any difference, each microbe concentrates its energy on making more microbes. As the microbe population increases, quorum-sensing molecules switch on the luciferase, the marine animal begins to glow dimly, and the bacteria and their host are more likely to survive because they no longer cast a shadow that could alert a predator. Quorum sensing has since been detected in many other kinds of bacteria.[38]

The Evolution of Mind

Willis Harman proposes a view of evolution that is, in some ways, the exact opposite of mainstream evolutionary thought. "Consciousness is not the end product of material evolution; rather, consciousness was here first."[39] Taking Charles Tart's argument further, Harman believes that mind, or consciousness, is primary, and that matter-energy arises, in some sense, out of mind. Indeed, Harman believes the ultimate stuff of the universe to be consciousness. "The physical world is to the greater mind as a dream image is to the individual mind. Ultimately the reality behind the phenomenal world is contacted, not through the physical senses, but through the deep intuition."[40] The latest developments in quantum physics on the role of the observer provide significant support for such notions (see chapter 4).

This primacy of consciousness seems important if we are to ascribe meaning to any consideration of the neurosphere. Consciousness is part of the substrate from which life arises. Life is a vehicle for consciousness and, in the human, a vehicle of ever-increasing complexity, success, and possibilities.

This view has been placed in historical context by philosopher William Irwin Thompson, who has thought a lot about biology in the context of history.[41] Thompson's arguments give consciousness a primary role as a matrix for human history. He emphasizes the importance of new "myths" in science that prefigure accepted theories, just as Teilhard's theories prefigured the rise of global technologies of communication like the Internet. Thompson wrote:

> [Like] the explosion of Renaissance magic that preceded the emergence of science and the modernist mentality, this so-called "New Age" (the recent movement of holistic health and spiritual questing) is probably the swan song of all the old ages.[42]

This is true, he posits, not because its particulars are provable science, but because it reflects the direction of human yearning.

In the face of recent and current chaos in the Balkans, Central Asia, Iraq, and Africa, Thompson's thinking also provides some optimism that seems to signal less rather than more unity. At the dawn of the Renaissance, for example, as people began to feel the strain of the emergence of an entirely new mentality, madness became a focus of societal attention, a phenomenon reflected in the literary creations of King Lear and Don Quixote. But madness then, and evil in the modern age, "is the unconscious emergence of the next level of organization. . . . Industrialization threatens the destruction of the biosphere, and this new evil serves in the formation of the next political level of Planetization."[43] Table 1 portrays Thompson's phases of human development.[44]

TABLE 1.

Phases of Human Development		
PHASE	ERA	CHARACTERISTIC MEDIUM
Culture	200,000-10,000 BC	image
Society	10,000-3500 BC	pictograph
Civilization	3500-1500 AD	writing
Industrialization	1500-1945 AD	print
Planetization	1945-?	digital

Mind extends beyond the pathways inside the body, says Thompson; and this larger mind knows much and has its way of knowing and learning:

> So, when we decide to resolve a problem by "sleeping on it," we recognize that there are modes of accessing insights and ideas . . . when we sense or intuit or pick up some message, we are still unconscious of the material, so the imagination reworks it. . . . The Imagination is therefore precisely this sensitivity to the other dimensions of Mind.[45]

In my view, the unconscious mind—or maybe just a larger unrecognized consciousness—has, throughout history, inspired individuals to create representations of what it knows to be true of the nature of reality. The recurring theme of these representations is unity or wholeness.

IMAGES OF WHOLENESS

Teilhard's concept of the noosphere was one in a long line of religious, artistic, sociopolitical, and scientific attempts to re-vision humanity as a species recognizing or moving toward its inherent wholeness and unity. A review of some of the attempts to envision this wholeness may help deepen the concept for us and perhaps operationalize some of its implications. Table 2 summarizes this progression.

TABLE 2.

Images of Wholeness		
TYPE	THEORY	EXPONENT
Religious	Noosphere	Teilhard de Chardin
Religious	Kabbalah	Esoteric Jews
Artistic	Dreamworld	James Joyce's *Finnegan's Wake*
Artistic	Sculpture	Willie Guttman
Scientific	Collective Unconscious	Carl Jung
Scientific	Gaia	James Lovelock
Scientific	Mycelial Mat	Ralph Abraham

Tibetan Buddhism

The fundamental message of Buddhism is that all matter and all thought, that is external and all that is internal, are fundamentally one substance.

> If it can be, that when you leave off all the conditions of phenomena, there shall remain no discriminating nature of mind, then both your mind and its Essence will have one individual and original nature, which would be their own and true reality.

> Universal mind is like a great ocean, its surface ruffled by waves and surges, but its depths remaining forever unmoved.[46]

Tibetan Buddhism, particularly as expressed in the *Tibetan Book of the Dead*, describes the mind as something distinct from the individual body.[47] "A subtle, mental level of life carries patterns developed in one life into the succeeding ones. . . . Once beings become conscious of the process, however, they can purposively affect their evolution through choices of actions and thoughts."[48] One of the goals of the *Book of the Dead* is to develop the ability to "die lucidly, to remain self-aware of what and where one is during these transitional experiences."[49]

Buddhists believe individual consciousness is fundamentally evolutionary. In Tibetan Buddhism, an individual consciousness moves through serial reincarnations. When individuals are sufficiently enlightened, they are no longer attached to individual bodies. After death, an individual consciousness may, in its enlightenment, merge with other minds in a deeper realm. More precisely, the individual consciousness recognizes the unity that was there all along. Buddhists do not equate this deeper realm with a neurosphere *per se*, but the direction of evolution in both systems of thought is similar. If a mind or individualized consciousness persists after death, surely it may merge with others in a neurosphere.

Buddhist practice trains individuals to recognize the fundamental unity within, an attitude I'll come back to in discussing how individuals may contribute to a more fully developed neurosphere. Using meditation, "you discover there is no fixed identity within yourself, no independent point of subjectivity. This discovery becomes the insight into selflessness, the door-way to liberation . . . greater mindfulness of one's whole system."[50] Later, we will also discuss why a move away from the notion that consciousness may have only a single point of subjectivity is crucial to experiencing the neu-rosphere.

One especially apposite Buddhist metaphor for unity is the Jewel Net of Indra:

> Imagine a vast net: at each crossing point there is a jewel; each jewel is per-fectly clear and reflects all the other jewels. In the net, the way two mirrors placed opposite each other will reflect an image ad infinitum. The jewel in this metaphor stands for an individual being, or an individual consciousness, or a cell or an atom. Every jewel is intimately connected with all other jew-els in the universe, and a change in one jewel means a change, however slight, in every other jewel.[51]

Curiously, my Internet Service Provider in Boulder, Colorado is Indra's Net, whose founders explicitly recognize the parallel between Indra's net of Buddhism and the Internet.

Transpersonal Psychology

Psychologist Ken Wilber attempted a Western, psychology-oriented inter-pretation of Buddhism and other types of Eastern mysticism in *The Atman Project*.[52] Wilber's treatment may help those put off by notions like reincarna-tion to obtain some insight from Buddhist models of unity. Wilber's model also emphasizes the evolutionary nature of consciousness and extends it to the societal realm.

According to Wilber, the basic stages of evolutionary development repeat at the individual and collective levels. These stages are:

Awareness of transpersonal realities

Transcendence of the ego

Unity with the higher level [53]

Wilber articulates these stages as "realms." In the Centauric realm, the mind transitions to an awareness of transpersonal realities. In the Subtle realm, the self is no longer bound to the ego but to its own higher archetype. In the Causal realm, the mind perceives what Wilber calls "final-God." And in the Ultimate realm, it merges with this "God" and all subject/object differences disappear.

In Wilber's view, the human fetus possesses a ground unconsciousness, where all deep structures exist as potential ready to emerge. The individual is not yet aware of this underlying unity. As the individual matures, however, deeper layers of the mind become visible through artistic imagination. In fact, they can best be reached through imagery, because verbal structures are insufficient. As Wilber puts it: "[I]mage is concentrated expression of the total psychic situation."[54] The process is not unlike asking a child to explain something in words rather than acting it out at a lower level.

Meditation is another technique for becoming aware of evolution and underlying unity—a technique that bypasses logic just as art does. This is why both art and meditation are easy to ridicule on a purely rational basis. Tolerance for ambiguity and the ability to live intensely in the present are aspects of Wilber's higher stages of growth. The individual is still aware of lower levels, and of past and future, but these are viewed as part of the *gestalt* of a higher-level "eternal present."

Characterizing the end goal of meditation by the Buddhist term "void" can be vaguely threatening. The goal of meditation is rather to experience an actual seamless reality, with no separation of subject and object. The Buddhist cycle of death and rebirth may be viewed instead as a metaphor for the gradual movement toward higher or deeper levels. While Wilber's personal psychological development mirrors higher levels evolving out of lower, it actually clears away obstructions to the experience of higher, or deeper, levels of unity that are always there.

Ultimately, Wilber believes that evolution equals self-realization through self-transcendence:

> The form of development, and the form of transcendence trace a curve from subconsciousness through self consciousness to superconsciousness, remem-

bering more and more, transcending more and more, integrating more and more, unifying more and more, until there is only that Unity which was always already the case from the start.[55]

To be fair, Wilber carefully considered the meaning of the Internet and concluded that it does not represent an emerging global consciousness in either his or Buddhist terms. I argue here only that his model of wholeness and unity is a modern take on a global view with a long lineage from which he himself takes inspiration.

Kabbalah

The notion of essential unity surfaces in Judaism in the form of the esoteric system of Kabbalah. All things emanate from God—called Ein-Sof, or the Infinite.[56] The world of energy and matter that we perceive emanates from the Ein-Sof through a series of stages. The first stage, the Sefirot, are aspects of the world of unity—intelligence, love, compassion, power. From the Sefirot, the "world of separate intelligences" derives. This is the world of distinct elements that surrounds us. The Kabbalist strives always to remember that these individual intelligences are the manifestations of an underlying unity.

Art and Wholeness

"Artists," Ezra Pound wrote, "are the antennae of the race." Art, like science, is perhaps always a reflection of the search for wholeness. Indeed, the work of sculptor Willy Guttman in the 1970s was an explicit portrayal of this concept. He created works consisting of metal blocks sliced in myriad shapes—like sashimi—without removing any of the original volume. His art focused on bringing out patterns that were always inherent in the whole.[57]

Perhaps the ultimate artistic view of wholeness is James Joyce's noted novel *Finnegan's Wake*. Its downside as art, of course, is its almost impenetrable writing style. Arguably, the only way to get the whole world and all of history in a book is through this kind of extreme literary compression. It speaks in the native language of the unconscious.

Jung's Collective Unconscious

Straddling artistic and scientific representations of wholeness, pioneering psychologist Carl Jung observed a set of common themes and images present in the dreams of his patients. He theorized that, in addition to the "personal unconscious" of each individual, all humans shared a "collective unconscious" consisting of universal images or archetypes. This collective unconscious is "identical in all men and thus constitutes a common psychic substrate of a suprapersonal nature which is present in every one of us."[58] Jung's student, Erich Neumann, characterized this "collective human background" as a "transpersonal reality," something that exists quite apart from any particular individual.[59]

Jung's theory is not empirically verifiable, yet it is intuitively appealing. It is possible to accept the theory, however, without seeing the collective unconscious as some actual substrate from which individuals draw meaning. Jung theorized that, just as instincts evolved from repeated learned behavior, so archetypes evolved from repeated inner experiences. They exist independently, in parallel, in different individuals. To fit the theory of the neurosphere to Jung's theory, we must articulate a mechanism for how these archetypes form a pool from which individuals can draw independently during the formation of their own specific genetic profile.

Following Jung, Joseph Campbell, scholar and popularizer of comparative mythology, traced common mythological themes and images across many different cultures, and viewed his work as evidence of the existence of a collective unconscious. The archetypal mother goddess or the hero archetype, he observed, are present in the mythology of many geographically dispersed cultures.

Mark Stefik, a principal scientist at Xerox PARC (Palo Alto Research Center), attempted a Jungian analysis of the technology and culture of the Internet in *Internet Dreams: Archetypes Mysts and Metaphors*.[60] Analyzing an assortment of metaphors ranging from the straightforward portrayal of the Internet as an "information superhighway" to more mythological images,

Stefik's comments are illuminating. Digital libraries, for instance, relate to Prometheus, the ancient keeper of knowledge, while email represents the archetypal messenger, Mercury. E-commerce mirrors the marketplace and the ubiquity of the trader, while virtual environments are reminiscent of Achilles and the adventurers and heroes of old. Stefik stops well short, however, of representing the Internet as a manifestation of a collective unconscious.

In general, psychologists and neurologists have not undertaken to operationalize Jung and perform quantitative research. However, scientists from an array of other disciplines have put forward models that approach the concept of wholeness from several other perspectives.

Science and the Divine Ground

Unified field theories of matter and energy increasingly implicate consciousness. Like the commonalities among world religions, different scientific descriptions of the ultimate nature of reality all seem to circle around common themes. Hyperspace appears as congealed humans and matter. Unified field theory sees gravity, nuclear strong force, nuclear weak force, and electromagnetism as different manifestations of a single field.

Implicit order makes atomic reality a blueprint for an implicit order, while in morphogenetic fields, organisms take the form of preexistent patterns. And finally, and most inclusively, digital data reduces all reality to a collection of zeros and ones.

In this context, humans are indeed part of a unified field. Whatever the root nature of reality—the divine ground—we are rooted in it because we are of one substance with it. The Greek Orthodox creed describes Jesus as "being of one substance with the Father, by whom all things were made." I am certain that Teilhard would have made that leap had he been educated on Mount Athos rather than in a Jesuit seminary.

The famous physicist Erwin Schrödinger arrived at wholeness by beginning with his conception of the "observer-created" universe. Schrödinger's thought experiments showed that the very action of observing an experiment altered its results, meaning that pure consciousness affects matter. He crystallized the implications of his breakthrough in the aphorism "Mind does not exist in the plural"— i.e., mind is not separate from matter. And since all matter is interconnected, so too is mind. Taking a slightly different approach, physicist David Bohm characterized atomic reality as the expression or explication of an implicit order or blueprint, whose resulting reality depends on the interpretation.

Biologist and writer Rupert Sheldrake put forward an evolutionary theory in which organisms select for characteristics that already exist among a given population, formed and solidified by repetition. He hypothesized a "morphogenetic field" that is generated by a critical mass of individuals—a field that then exists as a matrix from which new individuals draw genetic features.

Mathematician Rudy Rucker phrased the same concept in mathematical terms when he said that we are "squeezed off bubbles of hyperspace." Hyperspace, in mathematics, is a fourth-dimensional substrate of which we can perceive only the embedded three-dimensional forms. The potential always exists for any arrangement of matter within the flux of universe. In that sense, everyone is immortal, says Rucker.

Another mathematician who believes the evolution of humanity is moving in the direction of group mind is chaos theorist Ralph Abraham, who says:

> Now all we humans are connected, some more strongly connected than others by virtue of knowing their phone numbers or whatever, and we can see that if we connected all five billion minds on this planet, then we'd have a model for collective consciousness, or "the whole enchilada."[61]

Through his academic connections, Abraham was delighted to discover the Internet and then the World Wide Web. He noted that "[you] can have recreational use of the Net, like at cafes, but there's more than that. The explosive growth of the World Wide Web is happening now 'to save us from the Death Track,'" his term for the trends toward increased environmental degradation, extreme materialism, and increased intolerance. Abraham believes that telecommunication technology has increased the bandwidth of the mind's connections, and so has increased the overall intelligence of the species. Of course, Teilhard anticipated this very development, and called it noogenesis. He saw this as the resacralization of the world, the culmination of evolution. The World Wide Web is the material manifestation of Teilhard's vision.[62]

Abraham has made further provocative observations. As an amateur mycologist, he noted parallels between the World Wide Web and the Mycelial Mat—the web of fungal tendrils that connect underground over a wide area, but that show up as apparently separate, above-ground mushrooms. One such mat that was discovered a few years back in Michigan is now characterized as the largest living object on Earth.

Abraham believes it is no accident that, in terms of awareness of the inherent unity of humanity, there are certain mushroom-generated "altered states when we see those connections most clearly—in altered states we have our own experience of connectionism. And because the most information is in the connections, the whole thing is advanced by the efforts of the few shamans that do the stronger connections." This is a notion that will be revisited in chapter 5 as part of a consideration of the apparently differential progress of different ethnic, geographic, and income groups toward greater connectivity.

The View from Space

It was the techno-hippie philosopher Steward Brand (founder of the Well) who first asked the question: "Why haven't we seen a picture of the whole Earth yet?" He lobbied NASA, which finally produced a series of now-famous and beautiful images of the Earth taken from space. Brand used one as the cover for his *Whole Earth Catalog*, an icon of the environmental, back-to-the-land movement that was born in the 1960s. It proved a very powerful image indeed—and conjured up analogies of "Spaceship Earth." It was—and remains—symbolic of a range of concerns, uniting first a subculture and now even the mainstream of society

Astronauts, the icons of a human presence in outer space, experienced the view of the whole Earth first hand and were profoundly affected by it. Their experiences were documented in *The Overview Effect* by Frank White.[63] In interviewing the astronauts, White found a powerful, and largely unreported, spiritual side to space flight. For many astronauts, the experience of space flight changed their perceptions of space and time. The majority of them came away from the experience with what White terms a "global orientation." They had seen the Earth as a whole, and could no longer identify with border disputes or ethnic violence or nationalism. Such problems seem to stem precisely from an inability to experience the literal perspective of "wholeness" that the astronauts did. Moreover, they report coming away from their space flights with a very strong identification with ecological concerns. The "whole Earth" concept developed intellectually by Brand and others was experienced directly by these space travelers.

Apollo astronaut Edgar Mitchell experienced what he felt were profound mystical experiences while orbiting the Moon.[64] He was moved by the experience to form the Teilhardian-named Institute for Noetic Sciences, committed to documenting human potential and, in Maslow's terms, the farther reaches of human nature. Mitchell's fundamental perception from space was the unity of matter and consciousness. He founded the Institute to document the nature of consciousness as thoroughly and rigorously as science has done with matter. It is now a leading research organization representing the transpersonal view of human consciousness.

The venture into space served the United States, and maybe the world, as the Gothic cathedral served medieval society; everyone sharing in the spirituality of the great unifying experience. Then, as a sort of completion, man reached the Moon and enthusiasm for space flight faded. But the impact on society remained. Since the height of the space program, a number of scientific missions have been created that befit a species looking at itself and its planet as a unity. The Mission to Planet Earth is a multifaceted effort to use space-based observations to construct and maintain a comprehensive informational flow about the planet. The mission assists in the measurement of global health and, viewed from this book's perspective, provides a cybernetic feedback loop to humanity on its global body or nervous system.[65]

Futurist Willis Harman believes such information feeds humanity's abilities to solve global problems:

> Reprogramming the unconscious beliefs that block fuller awareness our creative/intuitive capabilities depends upon a key characteristic of the unconscious mind, namely that it responds to what is vividly imagined essentially as though it were real experience.[66]

The more information at hand, the more vivid and comprehensive the visualization, including hard-to-visualize goals such as a clean environment or world peace.

Gaia

Going one step beyond "whole Earth" imagery, biologist James Lovelock put forward the Gaia hypothesis. This states that the Earth, called Gaia after the mythic Earth goddess, "consciously" maintains planetary homeostasis. For example, Earth's magnetic field shapes ions of the solar wind into a protective aura. This appears to be an intelligent action taken by a living entity to protect itself. Similarly, all living systems are composed of subsystems that maintain internal order despite changes in their external environments. Living systems also act to protect against internal threats like infections. A few observers have noted sardonically that humans are analogous to destructive parasites that may ultimately have to be eliminated—perhaps through extreme measures like global warming—to preserve Gaia's homeostasis.

The Global Brain

Author Peter Russell's variation on the Gaia hypothesis characterized the entity as a single brain. In this metaphor, humanity serves as the cortex of the planet-as-brain. Russell proposed that humanity's ability to write and record experiences and knowledge and pass them down to new generations over time is an evolutionary trait analogous to sexual reproduction.

Russell also observed the fact that ten billion units seems to be a magic number for a new order to emerge in a number of contexts. For example, one living cell contains ten billion atoms; the human brain has ten billion nerve cells in the cortex.[67] So it may be extremely significant that the human population is estimated to approach ten billion within the next fifty years.

Star Maker

Sci-fi author and philosopher Olaf Stapledon put forth the most ambitious future history of human intelligence and its evolution in his novel *Star Maker*. In it, he posits unity as the end goal of evolution in the strongest possible terms.

Stapledon began his polemic (only barely a novel in form) with a human narrator who merges with a companion. "Our union of minds brought into being a third mind," he explains, "as yet intermittent, but more subtly conscious than either of us in the normal state."[68] This "third mind" encounters other composite beings:

> The mental unity of these little avians . . . was based on the unity of a complex electro-magnetic field, in fact on radio waves permeating the whole group. Radio, transmitted and received by every individual organism, corresponded to the chemical nerve current which maintains the unity of the human nervous system. Each brain reverberated with the ethereal rhythms of its environment; and each contributed its own peculiar theme to the complex pattern of the whole.[69]

Ultimately, these composite beings comprise the population of an entire world.

It is worth noting here that Stapledon took a Utopian view of the behavior of planetary beings:

> Tribal prestige, individual dominance, military glory, industrial triumphs lost their obsessive glamour, and instead the happy creatures delighted in civilized social intercourse, in cultural activities, and in the common enterprise of world-building.[70]

And Stapledon did not stop there (although I will). He further saw planets uniting into stars as organisms, then galactic minds, then nebular conscious-ness. Each stage is propelled by the same forces:

> [T]wo great longings, both of which were essentially religious . . . union with each other, and the desire to be gathered up once more into the source whence they had come [and so formed the cosmical mind]. . . . The many populations, teeming in the galleries of the many worlds, maintained their telepathic union. Intimately they knew one another in all their diversity. Together they supported the communal mind, with all its awareness of the whole vivid, intricate past of the cosmos, and its tireless effort to achieve its spiritual goal before increase of entropy should destroy the tissue of civiliza-tions in which it inhered.[71]

That goal is unity with the Star Maker:

> The eternally achieved perfection of the absolute spirit . . . the source of all cosmical light and life and mind . . . the eternal and perfect spirit which com-prises all things and all times, and contemplates timelessly the infinitely diverse host which it comprises.[72]

Then the purpose of life becomes clear: "[T]o have embodied for a moment the infinite and tumultuously creative spirit." And the goal of creation logi-cally follows: "[C]ommunity and the lucid and creative mind."[73]

The Thirst for Wholeness

Christina Grof saw the search for wholeness as a driving motivation for all individuals. After years of work as a therapist, she arrived at the impor-tance of wholeness in human motivation.[74] People are driven on a person-al level toward developing theories of wholeness. If they are not conceptu-al or verbalizing personalities, they manifest this desire in their life choic-es and day-to-day behavior. Grof documented many cases of individuals who failed to achieve wholeness in the family or in their personal realms, but who sought it in "save-the-world" causes. Even in the crass commer-cial world, merchandisers use spiritual symbols of wholeness (such as the whole Earth) to sell products, because people have a subliminal response to such messages.

Grof sees the proliferation of recovery programs for all types of addictions as a promising trend that we are waking up to our destructive attachments and attempting to deal with them. In true recovery work, individuals work to remove barriers between "small self" and "Deeper Self"—and sometimes you must to surrender your small self before you can know your Deeper Self.

Deeper Self, then, is Grof's term for the divine ground or collective unconscious. Her characterization of a *thirst* for wholeness suggests that a move toward the neurosphere is not only logical, but driven by strong individual motivations. I would go so far as to say that, just as the individual suffers addictions and other symptoms of a misdirected urge to wholeness, so may our society be lurching about in search of a global recovery through a global experience of wholeness. If all this sounds a bit mystical, well, we have indeed entered the realm of religion.

EVOLUTION AS RELIGION

I live in the rather liberal (we say "progressive"; others say "sinful") city of Boulder surrounded by an otherwise fairly conservative population. The Boulder community stands at the opposite ideological pole from Colorado Springs, home of Focus on the Family and other fundamentalist Christian organizations. Responding to the ubiquity of the metal magnet in the shape of the Christian fish symbol on many cars, many Boulderites have taken to sporting the same fish with little legs underneath and the word "Darwin" printed inside the creature's body. Like all intelligent humor, however, the juxtaposition of evolution and religion also carries deeper meaning.

The beliefs set forth in this book are the result of my own search for meaning. While I appreciate the ethical grounding embodied in the Christian Bible on which I was raised, I soon came to regard that Bible as allegory rather than actual history. Moreover, I came to see it as a book that is self-contradictory, and even ignorant or provincial. The core Christian belief—

that God made himself incarnate and died for our "sins," and that all we have to do is believe in him to live forever—seems like simple, childlike hope. I do not begrudge others that belief (although I do resent attempts to force those beliefs on others, particularly those weakened by sickness or personal tragedy), because I perceive that we all possess a fundamental need to impose a pattern of meaning on the world around us. The pattern I see is clearly an evolutionary one, and in that sense, the theme of this book is religious.

When I look at the history of religion, I am struck by the historical evolution of the interpretations of the feelings that can loosely be called religious experience. Ancient fertility cults developed into the Sun worship of the Egyptians. Sun worship extended to the tree and nature worship of the Celts and Druids. Worship of the dead flowed logically from the sacrality of the cycles of nature. Tribal chieftains became the chosen of God or his priests. From this came the concept of divine right and the merging of empire and church. In a naturalist reaction, the separation of church and state became moral law—a reaction that led, ironically, to the proclamation of the Death of God. It is this progression that has prepared the way for the rise of the neurosphere.

The neurosphere represents a mature religious view commensurate with the evolutionary stage at which we find ourselves. And if that is the case, then we'd do well to heed the words of erstwhile hippie philosopher Stewart Brand: "We are as gods, and might as well get used to it."[75]

CONSCIOUS EVOLUTION

Traditional religion in the United States has been under pressure from alternative spirituality for the last twenty years. "Conscious evolution" as a transformational possibility has grown to be a staple of the so-called New Age movement. It is easy to mock that view, as did William Burroughs: "Fish didn't one day just say, hey, I think I'll grow legs and become amphibian." But it seems clear that society is changing so fast and the ingress of novelty (to use Terence McKenna's phrase) is so great that it may be time to consider the possibility that we need to gain some kind of control over evolution. This may be easier to wrestle with if we stop thinking of evolution as strictly biological.

The End of Human Biological Evolution

Teilhard's theory presupposes an end to human biological evolution. Current evolutionary theorists tend to agree that we have adapted as much as we're going to, given current climatic conditions. Further evolution will either manifest in consciousness itself or in the "extended phenotype" proposed by biologist Richard Dawkins.

Dawkins believes that new kinds of evolution will appear in the "soup" of human culture. He coined the term *meme* to represent the unit of cultural transmission, analogous to the gene in biological transmission:

> Just as genes propagate themselves in the gene pool by leaping from body to body via sperms or eggs, so memes propagate themselves in the meme pool by leaping from brain to brain via a process which, in the broad sense, can be called imitation. . . . [The] old gene-selected evolution, by making brains, provided the "soup" in which the first memes arose. Once self-copying memes had arisen, their own, much faster, kind of evolution took off.[76]

The process is just as competitive as biological evolution, with memes competing for limited memory space in the brain, and perhaps more important, limited time and attention. And just as coadapted gene complexes may arise in the gene pool (such as compatible claws, guts, and sense organs in carnivores), so sets of memes may appear. For example:

> [If] a priest is a survival machine for memes (such as a meme for god-belief), celibacy is a useful attribute to build into him (otherwise marriage would interfere with his time spent building and influencing his flock.[77])

Dawkins' theories appear to provide a theoretical basis for studying the Internet and its communities as the "soup" of a new evolutionary stage in human existence. Douglas Rushkoff and others have noted how, if nothing else, the Internet acts as a lightning-fast replicator of memes of all types.

Institutions for Evolution

Psychologist Robert Ornstein and ecologist Paul Ehrlich presented a program for political activism based on a Teilhardian view of evolution in their book *New World New Mind*.[78]

> When you realize that all of human biological evolution happened before humanity's achieving its current mastery [agriculture, urbanization, mathematics, etc.] with the harvest of cultural evolution without a detectable corresponding physical evolution of the brain. . . . Cultural evolution, by giving us the ability to live on capital (food, fossil fuel) has made biological evolution completely inadequate as a way for human beings to adapt to their environments.[79]

Our institutions and societal structures are out of whack, say Ornstein and Ehrlich. "Our nervous system is attuned to short sharp changes." So we respond to "news," quick changes, and not to what's important in any long-term sense.[80] We "caricature" the world because we're unable to detect its subtler aspects, slow changes like overpopulation.[81] Since our nervous systems and the world now are mismatched, we must take conscious control of evolution. Ehrlich believes we must learn to use statistics that reveal long-term, slow changes. He suggests vehicles such as a "new world" segment on TV news, a "world box score" to show gradual changes, and a government foresight institute. The U.S. Congress, sadly and perhaps typically, decided to eliminate its Office of Technology Assessment, which had performed that foresight function.

On a personal level, Ornstein has, in other books, catalogued many techniques that have been developed to develop the mind more fully. For example, we may want to add the teaching of perceptual relativity to school curricula so we can understand why other cultures see things differently and thus are adaptive to their own circumstances.

Arthur Clarke, in his novel *Childhood's End*, argues that sometimes a new generation simply arises that embodies a new species, and all previous incremental attempts at change—such as those prescribed by Ornstein and Ehrlich—seem pale and impotent in comparison. The rise of a global mind may well be such an instance—the rise of a new species that, like some Eastern religions, will make clear the essential unity of all beings, and the indwelling of God in them and them in God.

Nevertheless, it may be possible to pave the way to the neurosphere consciously. To the extent that this evolutionary step is conscious and volitional, it makes sense to consider how individuals, groups, corporations, and governments are engaged every day in building the infrastructure for the neurosphere. This infrastructure comprises telecommunication and information technology and, especially, the Internet.

The Internet as Neurosphere

"Is it a fact or have I dreamed it—that, by means of electricity, the world of matter has become a great nerve, vibrating thousands of miles in a breathless point of time? Rather, the round globe is a vast head, a brain, instinct with intelligence!"

—NATHANIEL HAWTHORNE

I SPENT OVER TEN YEARS working for the cable television industry. It's an industry and a technology that, by a series of circumstances, seems to have risen erratically to its status of harbinger of the future. Yet, the manner in which it did so stands in considerable contrast to Ma Bell, a system that grew into a national institution in lockstep with the rise of 20th-century industrial civilization.

Cable television, by contrast, has grown in fits and starts. The industry began as a series of "community antennas," ways for households in out-of-the-way places to receive the newfangled broadcasting signals that emerged after World War II. Cable was a poor stepsister of broadcasting, built with borrowed money by hustlers whose first careers ranged from ranching to construction. Even after the invention of HBO and Ted Turner's revisioning of WTBS as a Superstation, cable companies were spurned by banks when they sought money for expansion. Cable pioneers then turned to junk-bond financiers like Michael Milken, whose venture capital paid off for both, despite some cable entrepreneurs, like Milken, ending up in jail.

When I came into the industry, the surviving pioneers were feeling the first flush of real financial success in the wake of industry deregulation in the mid-1980s. Almost immediately, these pioneers were beset by regulators seeking to reinstate price controls. Unfortunately, the cable companies had accumulated very little goodwill among their customers. Due to the ad hoc way in which the companies grew, technical reliability was spotty and customer service was almost an oxymoron. My lobbying colleagues and I sought positive stories to tell while representing a hated industry in Congress and before the FCC.

Starting in the early 1990s, technology became sexy. Spurred by my experience with the Well and early Internet explorations, I began to collect stories about innovative uses of cable technology. These ranged from remote arraignment of criminals from their jail cells, to tornado alert warnings in the heartland. I compiled these stories in a report called *The Future of Television*. What I was groping toward, without knowing it, was a description of the World Wide Web. Maybe I would have been more prescient had I not worked in the cable industry. Or maybe the organic nature of cable was part of the point I was trying to make. Either way, the advent of cable has served as my model for predicting how the infrastructure for the noosphere may arise.

BEYOND THE
GLOBAL VILLAGE

Marshall McLuhan proclaimed that the advent of digital technology "recreates the world in the image of a global village."[1] It has been axiomatic since McLuhan that telecommunication technology has indeed turned the world into a global village. However, it was partially true before McLuhan, for some parts of the population. The great colonial empires of the last 600 years, for better or worse, stitched together a connected world through ceaseless commerce in the mineral, chemical, and sometimes human resources of the lands they colonized. The sudden (relative to the scale of human existence) creation of an industrial civilization was built, in part, on the exploitation of the resources of far-flung global empires, but most of the population knew its economic neighbors only through the transmission of artifacts and the stories of explorers, soldiers, and colonists.

Those stories, however, could never capture the full reality—that is until television made the crucial difference. Television brought a vastly increased sensory bandwidth. A true human face was finally put on the stories of many lands far away from the industrialized West. My mother could say: "Eat your dinner; children in Biafra are starving." And I no longer had to rely on an abstract picture of those children—their distended bellies were in my living room on the nightly news on a regular basis.

Yet television remained a broadcast medium, a one-way exchange, for many years. It was hard to make the case that the people at the "other end of the pipe" were truly in communication with me or anyone else. McLuhan did say media are extensions of humans (e.g., television as eyes, computer storage as memory) just as cars are extensions of legs or knives are extensions of fingernails. Thus, because the mechanization of various physical organs has made social experience too much for the central nervous system to endure, we have created and set outside ourselves a model of the central nervous system in the form of communication media.[2]

I agree wholeheartedly that the totality of the world telecommunication system is an extension of the collective central nervous system and, more important, of the mind. Worldwide television gives us a prototype of a global mind, with satellite and other electromagnetic communication technologies serving as the neural pathways of the global brain.

McLuhan also noted that television and other "hot" media were low in participation. In part, this was because the information inflow was too much of a shock to the system to truly learn from it. Instead, the medium engendered a kind of somnambulism, encouraged by the flickering nature of television displays. However, McLuhan also envisioned a further evolution of media that would overcome their limitations. Ultimately, he projected, electronic technology would enable collective awareness without verbalization. Has his prediction come true? And if so, has that evolution given us a platform for a more encompassing wholistic view?

THE WIRED WORLD

Gordon Moore, founder of Intel, once declared that "the amount of power on a silicon chip doubles, and its cost is cut in half, every 18 months."[3] This principle, known as Moore's Law, has driven an extraordinary evolution in computing power, evident to most people in the personal computer revolution that started in the early 1980s. That rapid evolution was repeated more recently in the growth of computer networking technology, the tying together of computers over communication networks. That networking process was driven by the increasing power and declining cost of the hubs and routers, essentially computers themselves, that direct the traffic from computer to computer. Moore's Law thus proved to be true for the telecommunication industry as well.

It may be useful to talk about these trends, and the corporate and regulatory structures that emerge from them. These institutions bring us advanced telecommunication features and functions that will drive the transformation of a highly capable telecommunication and information infrastructure into something that is truly alive. The institutional and corporate factors driving the development of the infrastructure will, no doubt, draw even more attention as it becomes apparent that they themselves are part of an organism.

Bandwidth

Telecommunication capacity has seen explosive growth in the last twenty-five years, as a variety of businesses acknowledge the crucial competitive advantage it and other information technologies afford in a rapidly changing business environment. Increased processing power and connectivity have made economies of scale possible in a variety of businesses (think 7–11, Home Depot, Waste Management Inc., Citibank, Lockheed Martin, etc.).

The thirst for bandwidth from these corporate entities drove changes in the institutional structure of the telephone business. Companies like MCI emerged by finding ways to serve corporate appetites for bandwidth, and ultimately forced the breakup of AT&T. More recently, a new round of competitive telecommunication ventures arose to meet even faster expected growth in the thirst for bandwidth. Some of these companies failed financially because they overestimated that growth. Some, of course, failed through general corporate malfeasance. Nevertheless, bandwidth demand continues to grow.

For the purposes of my thesis, the explosive growth of telecommunication bandwidth obviously supports the notion of an emerging physical infrastructure for individuals communicating as cells in a global entity—neurons in a global brain. More, as well as cheaper, long-distance availability encourages inter-area communication. In turn, this encourages—inevitably, if sporadically—closer and more continuous ties between individuals.

Taking too broad a view of this, however, obscures how telecommunication really affects individuals. The corporate demand for bandwidth created easy profit opportunities (competing with 100-year-old telephone monopolies that had been, until MCI came along, a license to print money) and thus massive amounts of bandwidth were made available to business users. However, this bandwidth did not trickle down to residential telephone customers, who remained "cash cows" captive to a single provider. At the same time, regulators inhibited innovation in favor of keeping phone rates relatively stable.

Businesses structurally are able to adopt more and newer telecommunication capabilities because there are fewer individual points of connection. One fiber-optic line can serve one office building, and the cost of the fiber is shared among all the users in that location. However, single family homes tend to be slower to adopt the technology, because the cost of serving each home with high-capacity fiber has historically not provided a free-market, profit-driven business case. Service to single-family homes is known in the industry as the "last mile." Yet it is this connection—from large telecommunication "backbones" or superhighways to individual homes—that will encourage a true telecommunication-based nervous system.

Currently, every one of the 70 million U.S. cable subscribers is hooked into the global geosynchronous satellite web surrounding the planet like an electronic exoskeleton. More than 100 program networks uplink and downlink their merry way into our passive heads—not to mention a torrent of short-term satellite transponder usage for pay-per-view events, evangelist shakedowns, and guerrilla "disinfotainment."

At the turn of the century, cable modem technology, now called broadband, became a hotbed of development and frenzied investment speculation. A cable modem is the key piece of terminal equipment that allows cable subscribers to tap into high-capacity coaxial cables. In the years from 1996 to 1998, the speed of cable modems went from half a megabit per second to 30 mbps, the cost of modems went from over $500 to under $200, and equipment went from the size of a shoebox to a PC card that slips easily inside an existing personal computer. Industry research-and-development headquarters, CableLabs, put the finishing touches on a worldwide cable modem standard in early 1999. This is where the action is. What can we do with a wire that, for a long time, was thought by the most creative minds in the world to be suited only for delivering popular television shows? The answer was, and is, the Internet.

Surveys of early experiences with cable modems indicate that their high speed and constant access led to usage patterns different from ordinary Internet use. Among the findings:

Cable-modem users are on the Internet four times as much as phone-modem users.

Constant access led to more frequent use of the Internet to look for information.

Usage integrated into household tasks such as checking the weather or shopping.

Users are more likely to access multiple times during the day for short periods.

Women and children have become primary household users of the Internet.

Usage has moved from evening hours to all times of the day.

Usage has moved from offices/spare rooms to kitchen/family rooms.[4]

Other Paths to Home

Cable is just one of multiple telecommunication paths into the home. Others include telephones, wireless hotspots, satellite and microwave signals, portable media like CDs and DVDs, and simple electrical utility wires. While cable may be the best positioned of these, in a business, technological, and institutional sense, to provide high bandwidth to the home, it is clear that "wi-fi" is the fastest growing newcomer to the market. With wi-fi, almost any individual, in either their home or business location, will shortly have very high-bandwidth connections at their fingertips. Before long, very high-band-width wireless connections will be available to anyone carrying the right piece of handheld equipment.

A lag always exists between the cost of wireless telecommunication, because all over-the-air communication is plagued with having to operate in a very hostile environment—the ambient atmosphere. Techniques for preserving the integrity of signals from a variety of impairments and interferences are being developed rapidly, but telecommunication carriers who deliver signal over a shielded wire still have much more control over their environment. Moreover, there is great competition for over-the-air spectrum, as there are many functions that preclude a direct, stable wired connection. Television and radio broadcasts, cellular phones, CB radio, ship-to-shore transmissions, and many other types of communication compete for what is ultimately a scarce resource—usable over-the-air electromagnetic spectrum.

Even in this market, however, new technologies for sharing bandwidth among multiple users, such as dynamic frequency hopping, move us even further in the direction of communication channels that carry as much information as a global brain might need to accurately represent reality in all its complexity.

The Commercialization of the Internet

The year 1993 was the first in which Americans bought more personal computers than television sets. This was also the year that cable television companies started talking to computer companies about joint ventures. It was a heady time in the cable industry, climaxing with the blockbuster announcement that Bell Atlantic and TCI were merging, and IBM and Silicon Graphics were waiting in the wings to sell them the latest computer technology.

The resulting Internet boom came out of nowhere, albeit a nowhere that was thirty years in the making. In 1993, the new Clinton administration set out their agenda for a National Information Infrastructure. This agenda was ambitious and inclusive:

> People would be able to live almost anywhere and "telecommute" to work on an electronic highway.
>
> The best schools, teachers, and courses would be available to all students, without regard to geography, distance, resources, or disability.
>
> Health-care information and other important social services would be available online, without waiting in line, when and where you needed them.
>
> Private-sector investment, encouraged by appropriate tax policies, would extend the "universal service" concept to ensure universal access.
>
> Technological innovation and new applications would grow, supported by government research programs and grants.
>
> The NII would evolve into a "network of networks," allowing users to transfer information easily and efficiently.
>
> Information would be secure; networks would be reliable.
>
> The government would improve management of the radio-frequency spectrum, protect intellectual property rights, and provide easy access to government documents.
>
> Governments would be able to coordinate action and share information.[5]

Clinton relied, in part, on the continuing development of the Internet—evolved from the patchwork of government and research networks known as DARPAnet—as a means to avoid the kind of "big government" spending that was clearly out of favor. The Internet as we know it today is a network of networks that are connected only by adherence to a common protocol or interconnection standard known as TCP/IP. While it had been the private playground of government and academia, who used it for sending large chunks of research information, it had a lot of spare capacity that could be also used for playing games, figuring out new applications, or just chatting about non-work-related topics.

This network of networks was fostered by the National Research and Education Network (NREN) program; the National Science Foundation oversaw its backbone, known as NSFnet. Beginning in the early 1990s, NSFnet was transformed into a semi-commercial venture. Under contract to the National Science Foundation, a consortium of IBM, MCI, and Merit Network Inc. (the educational network provider for the state of Michigan) took over its operation. This consortium, known as ANS, constituted the first exploration of privatization of the Internet—an experiment that led to further commercial innovation.

The value of the Internet to a range of nontechnical types became increasingly apparent. Researchers invented tools that helped people find and use information. These were relatively elegant solutions overlaid on a set of computers and information managers who didn't think in user-friendly terms. But that all changed with a group of researchers who created a standard way to present information called Hypertext Markup Language, or HTML, and a way to look at that information called Mosaic, the first Web "browser." That team moved on to start a company called Netscape, and the rest is not just history, but absolute mania.

"The dream behind the Web," Tim Berners-Lee observes, "is of a common information space in which we communicate by sharing information. Its universality is essential: the fact that a hypertext link can point to anything, be it personal, local or global, be it draft or highly polished." But, he continues, "[t]here was a second part of the dream, too, dependent on the Web being so generally used that it became a realistic mirror (or in fact the primary embodiment) of the ways in which we work and play and socialize."[6] It is the extent to which one can implement this second part of the Internet dream that will determine how successful we are in helping to manifest the neurosphere.

Information Haves and Have-Nots

This is a phrase that politicians uttered countless times during the heyday of the National Information Infrastructure, using the catchphrase to generate digital pork-barrel projects for home districts. Many of these programs were well-meaning attempts to get computers into schools in the poorest neighborhoods, but most programs died out over time as schools and libraries realized they were unable to keep up with an obsolescence cycle of around two years—a task for which help was not forthcoming from Silicon Valley, which moved on to greener sales pastures.

The ironic thing is that Moore's Law is nondiscriminatory. Despite the best/worst efforts of Bill Gates and Andy Grove to squeeze monopoly profits out of the wealthiest third of the population through endless hardware upgrades and software bloat, the Internet generated new business models that drove computer prices under $1,000. Then marketing pressures encouraged companies to practically give away computers, as long as their owners agreed to surf the Internet through proprietary browsers that carried advertising banners galore.

The spread of technology in the underdeveloped world will happen quickly as well—indeed, much faster than traditional top-down international aid programs could ever hope to drive. A new bank called Grameen Bank has pioneered the concept of microlending. They began by lending as little as $30 in Bangladesh, or just enough capital to get a small business off the ground. Grameen started a project called GrameenPhone, which has distributed 4,000 cellular phones to villages. The owners of the phones in each village borrow money to buy the hardware, then sell individual calls to their neighbors and use the income to repay their loans.[7]

Another example is Freeplay, a company with deceptively simple radios and other appliances powered by almost frictionless windup springs that don't require broadly deployed electrical-power infrastructures. The appliances usually sell for under $100 per unit, which allows individuals in the poorest of undeveloped countries to have access to them. A United Nations

Development program recently used them to broadcast election results to the people of Liberia.

It is interesting that the Freeplay company was started with explicit social goals by its South African founders in the wake of the end of apartheid. British humanitarian Terry Waite serves on the company's board, perhaps as a result of his years as a hostage in Lebanon. For four years, Waite was without human contact to give him any sense of the outside world. Then he got a small, battery-operated radio. "I was terrified that when the batteries died, the guards would not replace them, and I'd be back in total isolation. There are millions of people in this world who are in similar situations—cut off from the flow of information."[8] The company is working on windup-powered computer and cell-phone products. Founder Rory Stears says simply: "This is how the Internet will get to Africa."

THE RISE OF THE WORLD WIDE WEB

As we have seen, the Internet really began as a secret project of the U.S. Defense Department. The primary driver behind its creation was the fear of nuclear war. Researchers were set the task of figuring out just how to preserve military communication channels after a nuclear attack, an attack it was assumed would destroy many phone lines and disable other parts of the communication infrastructure. The Internet was not designed to be the most efficient communication network, but simply one that could transmit a message from point A to point B even if the primary, secondary, and tertiary preferred paths were not available.

Researchers made various improvements to the Internet's techie interfaces over time, and the wealth of university talent exposed to it made it only a matter of time before someone came up with a vehicle for navigating the network. Mosaic, the first browser for the World Wide Web and precursor of

Netscape, caused a run-up of Internet stocks in 1998–1999 that was unprecedented. And although that wave finally broke, it did not roll back very far.

These developments marked a quantum leap in bringing information technology to a broad audience. Moreover, it is reasonable to speculate that the new interface improved the quality as well as the quantity of interaction. As Marcos Novak has commented: "Cyberspace stands to thought as flight stands to crawling."[9] Indeed, he term "Internet years" was coined to describe the speed of changes that have occurred in just the past five years. It may not be too early to look for evidence of increased quality in certain types of communication, as reflected in some very high-profile and successful Internet services.

Aggregating Eyeballs

The august Time Inc. was one of the first large corporate entities to establish an outpost in cyberspace. Pathfinder was a collection of sites that mirrored Time's portfolio of magazines—*Time*, *Sports Illustrated*, *People*, etc. The site was launched more to display technology leadership than to make money, but it was one of the first initiatives to make the point that advertisers would pay for the privilege of running ads in a new "place" where lots of people were looking.

At first, it was enough to simply aggregate eyeballs. Over time, however, advertisers began to question the value of the advertising. They began to develop more sophisticated measures of marketing effectiveness and asked questions such as: Are visitors "clicking through" an ad to go to the advertiser's own Web site, and possibly initiate an actual sale?

While advertising on the Internet is still an art rather than a science, it is clear that it already offers advertisers something they can't get with traditional television advertising—interactivity. An interactive experience is more engaging than a passive viewing experience, especially one undertaken while the viewer is in the tranquil state characterized by alpha brainwaves. Studies show an improvement in retention and increases in ultimate sales resulting from interactive ads. Further, a commercial transaction resulting from an engaging inter-active experience keyed by advertisement can form a significant part of a general experience that knits people together.

Electronic Publishing

A popular and moderately successful category of commercial Web site is online magazines or news sources. Increasingly, people track live, unfolding stories on the Web, not content to wait for next-day newspapers or even television coverage. Television networks must not, except for events of gravest interest, disturb the schedules they've trained their audiences to expect, lest their advertisers become nervous.

This movement of breaking news to the Web is a harbinger of how a global organism can absorb information about its environment. In responsiveness and global coverage, existing Web news sites are approaching the kind of capability a living entity demands. Where they still fall short is in depth of coverage. Some special-interest sites provide in-depth coverage and historical context for topics ranging from ethnic conflict to weather. But too many commercial sites like the *New York Times* charge for access to top level stories, and charge even more for access to archives and information more than two weeks old.

There is a lesson here about a conflict between the goals of unity and communication and the interests of business models that motivate media companies to make information scarce. Many Internet theorists—among them Stewart Brand—take the position that "information wants to be free." In a neurosphere, information circulation is as vital as the flow of blood is to a biological organism.

E-Commerce

Old-line companies like Time Inc. looked to advertising to fund their online businesses, because that was the model they understood as newspaper and magazine publishers. The dizzying rise of companies like Amazon.com and eBay confirmed the practical benefits of migrating business-to-consumer commerce to the virtual world. Yet those companies also made the point that e-commerce didn't entail just taking some physical activity and moving it intact to cyberspace. E-commerce is driven by a form of interaction that is more complex and multilevel than traditional commerce. Not only can you buy recorded music on the Web, you can listen to selections before buying, exchange messages with other people who have reviewed the recording, or discover the artist's connections or collaborations with musicians with whom you are already familiar. The Internet creates a richer communication experience as part of a business transaction.

This interactivity was integral to the Napster phenomenon, which was soon swept away by the mania of Free Music. Copyright owners fought back hard, in the process labeling every downloader a pirate. They could not admit that some peer-to-peer music sharing was exactly that—sharing between friends that ultimately led to increased, not decreased, sales. It took Steve Jobs, through iTunes, to get it right. He pioneered a viable commercial service with compensation for artists, that allowed consumers flexibility, convenience, and access to a community built around the music.

As demand increases for e-commerce support, many companies are developing tools for electronic financial transactions. Adaptations of software programs like Microsoft's Money or Intuit have appeared and security technologies have been developed to protect against online fraud. In mid-1999, the first banks were chartered that operated exclusively on the Internet. For example, at Wingspan Bank, some loans are approved or rejected in less than a minute.[10] These watershed events reaffirm the notion that money itself is ultimately information. This is a model of wholeness that posits a common substrate of binary data or information. It is hard to imagine anything in these days of *homo economicus* that will better motivate people to unite than a well-lubricated financial system based on the Internet.

Chat Rooms

Another Web-based business model creates central locations where consumers come to communicate with each other. Chat, real-time "conversation" between two typists, is an activity that is propagating like a virus on the Internet, particularly among the young. The kind of considered, leisurely conversation that I first experienced within the Well made me view chat as superficial and banal at first, although the Well has had this feature, called the "send," since the 1980s. Yet, like any small talk, chat is a way in which relationships can be built over time. It is also arguably closer to the way a group mind would function, exchanging messages in near-real time rather than with the delay associated with conferencing and building deeper relationships cumulatively over time. Instant messaging is another version of real-time communication over the Internet whose quantum growth has sparked fierce competition between Microsoft and America Online.

Networked Video Games

Video games are clearly a major mode of communication among (mainly) teenagers. Web sites like HEAT.NET and Total Entertainment Network have experienced huge growth despite their user experience being inferior to arcade games where two players can compete directly against one another. The current Internet provides low-speed and high "latency," long lags that degrade the gaming experience. As cable modem speeds become commonplace, however, and guaranteed quality of service emerges, the experience these sites offer will catch up with their highly motivated customers.

Much has already been written that is highly critical of the immersive nature of video games. It may be, however, that the viability of a group mind is based in part on an individual's willingness to blur ego boundaries and allow his or her consciousness to mingle with another's. The multiplayer video game is a clear example of this blurring of boundaries.

Current game developers are adding features that allow players to chat with each other while playing, and advances in graphic technology are pointing to even more immersive environments. It is no accident that Sony calls the silicon chip that powers its latest game machine "The Reality Engine," while Sega calls their game engine the "Emotion Chip."

Monetizing Community

When it comes to breaking down boundaries between individuals, there's nothing like living together in a community. Microsoft's Sidewalk sites, America Online's Digital City sites, and others have created information spaces about particular geographic areas. They trade in information in order to attract eyeballs, but are really focused on selling advertising, gaining sales commissions, or otherwise delivering those eyeballs to merchants.

These sites stand in contrast to the Boulder Community Network and others that seek to create an information space that parallels both the physical and personal topography of a given area. The stated goal of a similar network in the Washington, D.C. area called the MetaNetwork is "to close the gap between the human condition and the human potential." That may not support a business, but it might support a community. The question seems to be whether there is a middle ground that generates a sustainable business model, while retaining the power to knit together a real community.

Future Web Growth

Between 1998 and 1999, it seemed that no forecast of Web growth was too extravagant. Les Vadasz, Senior Vice President at Intel Corporation, foresees one billion interconnected computers world-wide within ten years at current rates of growth. Web access is currently available to half of existing computers, but that number is growing exponentially. We can expect that almost all PCs will be connected to the Internet in the next ten years. Once again, it seems clear that the physical infrastructure of the neurosphere—the blood, bones, and muscle of a global entity—will be in place very soon.

IMPLICATIONS OF THE WEB

On the Well, participants like myself believe the Internet and World Wide Web are living, organic things, but we don't often discuss it for fear of spoiling the magic we perceive. Or perhaps we just don't want to appear too pretentious. However, the following post, by Steve Silberman (digaman) on Friday, November 24, 1995, is worth recounting:

> The Net is "organic" because we who build it are organic and it is a reflection of its builders. Not only its builders' egos and ambitions, but the subconscious of its builders as well, and the parts of our own consciousness that lay beyond the flashlight of awareness.
>
> Wouldn't it be strange for bees to consider themselves part of nature but their hives to be artifice? We've finally found a "beeswax" that is nearly infinitely pliable. You can turn what the Net is made of into stimulus for nearly any sense modality. (Though you can't yet create life-forms with it—and smell is underutilized.) We are building the infinitude inside ourselves outside ourselves, as best we can. It is not surprising that the Net itself appears to be "alive," even autonomous. It's sculpted of mind-stuff.

In *The Millenium Myth*, philosopher Michael Grosso writes:

> Today, after more than a century of electric technology we have extended our central nervous system itself in a global embrace, abolishing both space and time as far as our planet is concerned. . . . The root of this fascination is the promise of control over the world by the power of the will.[11]

Prior to becoming something of an Internet personality, Well denizen and author Howard Rheingold wrote a book called *Tools for Thought*. The book was a popular treatment of a number of computer-industry theorists who viewed computers not only as an extension of man in McLuhan's sense, but specifically as extensions of the human mind. The use of computers, Rheingold claimed, was a new phase in intellectual life. Interaction with a computer program authored by a human constituted, essentially, interaction with one's own thoughts. Further, as the computer relieves the load on short-term memory, it enables better quality of thought focused on complexity. Inasmuch as the nature of human growth means an increase in complexity,

Rheingold saw the computer as an extension of the human mind emerging, on demand, as a way to manage this complexity. Computers were not about automation, but augmentation—and that augmentation is a fundamental alteration of consciousness and how it works.

Rheingold further saw the value of online communities in early efforts such as EIES or Prodigy in the late 1970s. These early systems allowed the creation of commonalities of interest that went beyond accidents of birth and geography. In my view, the combination of computer-enhanced minds and telecommunication-enhanced connectivity constitutes the early stages of a more integrated, and ultimately conscious, organism.

If there is a collective mental ecology, what would its characteristics be? Gregory Bateson once attempted to characterize what made something alive. Living things, he noted:

Have complex organization of multiple systems that interact

Take in and use up energy, later releasing it in another form

Grow, develop, and change to better suit utilitarian needs

Reproduce with variation

Show these variations based on heredity, mutation, and evolution

Are able to adapt to their environment to various degrees

Respond to stimulus

Let's see how well the Internet and the World Wide Web fit these characteristics.

Have complex organization of multiple systems that interact: Interconnection of various smaller networks is the *sine qua non* of the Internet. The Internet Protocol (TCP/IP) and the routing tables built into the complex data-communication switching equipment are the roadmap of how multiple systems interact.

TAKE IN AND USE UP ENERGY, LATER RELEASING IT IN ANOTHER FORM: The telecommunication infrastructure over which the Internet's content flows certainly consumes energy, and releases it in the form of heat by-product. At another level, the Web absorbs the attention and energy of millions of people, and constantly reflects that energy in the second-to-second reshaping of information and activity that occurs on the Web, or drives action in the "real" world, like flurries of "daytrading" in the stock market.

GROW, DEVELOP, AND CHANGE TO BETTER SUIT UTILITARIAN NEEDS: Recent years have seen the refinement of the Internet as a tool for business and a tool for more efficient individual consumer behavior, e.g., e-commerce. On a more fundamental survival level, disenfranchised people such as the Mayan Zapatistas or the Kurds have founded virtual nations online that serve as a crossroad for their people in diaspora or for sympathetic outsiders.

REPRODUCE WITH VARIATION: Some may argue that a machine that builds a replica of itself is not really alive. If you define the Internet as merely its physical infrastructure, the same criticism applies. But if you see the Internet as the aggregate of human behavior played out there, then you constantly see new forms of interaction supplementing or superseding the old—all the activities create demand for more extensive physical telecommunication infrastructure, and so the Internet reproduces itself, both body and soul.

SHOW THESE VARIATIONS BASED ON HEREDITY, MUTATION, AND EVOLUTION: This is a tougher criteria; but Richard Dawkins' concepts of the meme and the extended phenotype certainly apply on the Web. If you believe they are signs of life, then you can extend that view to the Internet as well.

ARE ABLE TO ADAPT TO THEIR ENVIRONMENT TO VARIOUS DEGREES: The Internet's very genesis flowed from a desire to withstand nuclear attack—how adaptive can you get?

RESPOND TO STIMULUS: There are many examples of swift generalized response to events reflected on the Web. Stock-market gyrations, public spectacles like police car chases, notorious trials, and more have brought otherwise robust, high-speed Internet connections to their knees. Web-specific event programming like the Victoria's Secret lingerie fashion show tied to the Super Bowl can drive enormous amounts of traffic as well. These events and their attendant growth in appetite for bandwidth causes market responses in the deployment of additional network infrastructure.

This short list is hardly rigorous or dispositive. Nevertheless, it does suggest that the Web acts increasingly like a living thing.

The Planetary Nervous System

With the bandwidth and personal interface in place, the kinds of connections to other people described in embryonic form in chapter 1 can begin to reach their fullest flower. The concerns shared and expressed will be those of the individuals who are so connected. I discussed above the growth of the Web as a real-time, in-depth (sometimes) news source that may serve as the information life blood of the neurosphere. You can also imagine that certain types of information—types that are important only to those who "think globally"—may be incorporated as a kind of utility information for all who are connected.

The Web site *www.nerosphere.org* is one that I check in with daily. It is intended to raise to a conscious level the kind of noospheric activity that may be emerging without my notice. If earth and human merge as part of a single entity, then the environment section gives me a "medical" status report on my weather, air quality, and other descriptive data. If the Internet is part of the infrastructure of a global brain, then the State of the Internet tells me the condition of the pathways around me and the value my fellow humans are placing on the connections. And with NASA's Destination Earth, the Space Shuttle, and other sites reporting from the eyes and ears we have placed in the atmosphere, I can experience through immersion an expanded sense of what is "local."

Here are some of my own links to the neurosphere:

THE WORLD RIGHT NOW

EarthCam (*http://www.earthcam.com*): An extensive geographically indexed list of live outdoor images from around the world.

Search Engine Subconscious (*http://www.google.com/press/zeitgeist.html*): A ticker of which terms are being employed by users of the search engine Google.

VIRTUAL COMMUNITIES

The Well (*http://www.well.com*): My geography-independent community.

Boulder (Colorado) Community Network (*http://bcn.boulder.co.us*): My geographic community.

STATE OF THE INTERNET

Weather Report on the Internet Itself (*http://www.weather.uci.edu*): How well is information flowing across the Internet?

Realtime Spot Market for Telecomm Bandwidth (*http://www.band-x.com*): An indirect indicator of how much we are communicating with each other.

General Internet Statistics (*http://www.isoc.org/internet/stats*): Links to Internet stats, compiled by the International Internet Society.

HEADLINES

National (*http://www.cnn.com*)

International (*http://www.usatoday.com/news/world/nw1.htm*)

Greece (*http://athensnews.dolnet.gr/grknews/grn.htm*): Country of my ancestors.

ENVIRONMENT

Boulder Weather (*http://www.crh.noaa.gov/den/awebphp/forecast.php*): Local weather.

Destination Earth (*http://www.earth.nasa.gov*): National weather

Shuttle (*http://www.osf.hq.nasa.gov/shuttle/futsts.html*): Which of us is out there monitoring the world?

Interplanetary (*http://www.jpl.nasa.gov:80/galileo/countdown/mclock.html*): An even broader perspective.

The World Right Now sites provide a window on global consciousness, as expressed through people's words, dreams, and desires. These are, in turn, expressed in online communities, in search engines, or in the stories they tell. This is enhanced by a burgeoning array of digital cameras that are being piped directly onto the Web.

Writer Alan Moore created a character who uses multichannel cable television to populate a wall-sized video mosaic that is parsed by intelligent computing power to identify recurring images and themes. These are then used to guide the character's investment strategies. Reality has followed fiction, as several companies now seek to bring the processing power of computers to bear directly through digital video streams. This has allowed viewers to search on images and extract meaning. So if we have more global video coverage, will this really initiate an interconnected awareness?

MTV guiding genius Robert Pittmann speaks, perhaps self-servingly, of a sort of image intelligence that is a positive quality of what he calls "TV babies."[12] TV babies "read" a picture on television, understand body language, understand context (Is this a news program or satire?), and recognize production time frames (rerun or original) at a glance. Further, they have mastered "multitasking." They can do homework, watch television, and listen to the radio at the same time: "It's as if information from each source finds its way to a different cluster of thoughts. And at the end of the evening, it all makes sense."

This view suggests a new multidimensional language that perhaps should be studied and incorporated into educational approaches, rather than reflexively dismissed as it surely is by "back-to-basics" advocates. On the other hand, this new approach should not replace teaching of fundamental reading and other core skills.

An ongoing concern has been the fact that this world-encompassing info-structure is comprised of pieces of technology that were once turned to self-defeating ends by some. Yet, taken as a whole, they can actually serve as tools to achieve long-sought political justice. Soviet spy pictures are now for sale in this strange, post–Cold War world.[13] Perhaps they can be repurposed to document and publicize atrocities as they occur, when such things as prison camps can no longer be hidden by various national security interests.

Some voice Orwellian concerns about a burgeoning surveillance culture. The other edge of that sword, however, is that we may choose to monitor ourselves for our own purposes, with personal privacy intact to some extent. More accurately, we surrender privacy to the degree that we choose, in exchange for a corresponding degree of participation in the larger infosphere. Fortunately, the rapid development of personal technology makes it easier for individuals to opt in or out, deploying technology for their own protection as well as for greater participation.

HUMAN/NETWORK INTERFACES

High-capacity networks are now available that connect individuals to each other. Predictably, the human interfaces used to take advantage of those connections have a huge impact on communication, as does the wide array of technologies used to access and, over time, internalize the information matrix that will ultimately manifest the neurosphere.

Unfortunately, the human interface is lagging far behind the bandwidth and processing power gains that would otherwise have enabled seamless, user-friendly connectivity. With software prices still beyond the reach of 60 percent of American households and annual upgrades of bloated programs forcing people to climb steep learning curves, potential gains in productivity, performance, and storage have gone unrealized.

Fortunately, the Internet favors a model of thin clients: PC's that are lean and fast. By the end of 1998, computers selling for under $1,000 were the fastest-growing category of PC, and computers at consumer electronics price points (i.e., under $300) were within reach. Thus the same technology that enables thinner clients also enables the migration of computing intelligence into all sorts of devices, not just computers. Given the trends in computing intelligence and in bandwidth to the home and other locations, we can profile the technology the average citizen may have available to augment an interconnected consciousness.

Moreover, we can map developments in communication and information technology onto the functions of consciousness. The brain's functions distinguish the human from other organisms. In any human group consciousness, each individual will serve as a brain cell or synapse in a larger brain. These human components of the Internet mind will need access to and control of technology so they can plug into and be an integral proactive part of the global nervous system—part of the infrastructure of the neurosphere.

Processing

When people dubbed computers "electronic brains," they were referring to a machine's ability to perform calculations, the ability to take information from several sources and do something with it to solve a problem or complete a sequence. For individuals to serve as nodes in a group brain, they must also have some amount of processing power. In this age of "information overload," it may already be apparent that individuals will need even more processing power than the existing human brain provides. Supplemental processing power is now available to people in 40 percent of U.S. households, and probably close to 75 percent when you factor in computers available to people at their jobs. These are general-purpose computers that increase our efficiency in writing, arithmetic, and other basic functions.

An interesting aspect of software engineering has been the development of so-called groupware, which brings to bear the processing power of several individuals on a single project. The Internet has made possible massive parallel processing projects. One example is the SETI@Home Project, a cooperative effort to process astronomical information relating to the search for extraterrestrial intelligence.[14] The project uses the capacity of thousands of personal computers to examine incoming signals for patterns that could indicate intelligence. The individual PCs then upload results to the Internet, effectively harnessing the processing power of many thousands of individuals worldwide in a single effort.

The success with which PCs have penetrated society has led to a further implementation of Moore's Law. Chips that once powered entire computers are now found in remote controls, microwave ovens, and telephones. The day when they may be surgically implanted in individuals to supplement their own gray matter may not be far off.

Memory

Although the brain is an amazing storage device, it quickly became apparent that it cannot begin to approach the storage capacity of a computer. The human memory, though impressive, is limited. It seems to retain best those things that carry the most, often random, emotional impact. As we grow and change, things we thought we had learned seem not to have been permanently imprinted in our limited personal memories. Computers may provide a means for storing those many things that pass through our experience, but don't acquire relevance until later in our lives.

The growth of computer memory, on the other hand, has been geometric. Mainframe computers were developed that efficiently stored information in increasingly smaller spaces. Then a generation of computer advances brought us minicomputers. And finally, a new era dawned in the garage of Steve Jobs and Steve Wozniak with the birth of the personal computer.

As libraries and other storehouses of information become digital, the line between what we store in our brains and information that can be accessed electronically is blurring. There is a growing list of databases that are making advances in information and medical technology as readily available to us as if they resided in our heads. Lexis Nexis (*http://www.lexis-nexis.com*) puts news, commentary, and legal decisions at our fingertips, while Medline Plus (*http://medlineplus.gov*) gives easy access to medical information. The Library of Congress Project (*http://www.loc.gov*) is opening up many diverse sources of information, just as Project Gutenberg (*www.gutenberg.org*) is making available electronic texts of works from the Bible to *Moby Dick*. The Corbis Photographic Archives (*http://www.corbis.com*) bring a stunning array of images into our lives, while the Encyclopedia Brittanica Web site (*http://www.eb.com*) puts a large portion of all accumulated human knowledge at our fingertips.

Aural and Visual Communication

Individual intelligence is determined in part by the number of interconnected neurons in each brain. Telecommunication these days is all about extending interconnectivity and interoperability—between individuals and between networks of individuals. Tools like local and long-distance telephone, data communication, Internet access, in-home networks (wired or wireless), and satellite communication are increasingly available to more and more individuals.

Likewise, a wide array of display devices are increasingly available to deliver the results of directed or autonomous digital processing. Video monitors are evolving from tube and solid-state designs into versatile flat-screen displays. Video monitors, preferably high-definition digital, can now be mounted in different parts of the home, all connected to high-speed data connections. Head-mounted displays bring the technology another step closer to being internalized. And there may laser-based, retinal projection screens available in the not-so-distant future. Thus visual information—a key input for any organism—is rapidly being built into the infostructure.

Command and Control

The invention of tools enabled early humans to control their external environment. The invention of the mouse at the Xerox Palo Alto Research Center was perhaps one of the most important advances made in human tools in generations. It began the intuitive age of "point-and-click" controls for personal computers. Consumer electronics remote-control technology took some time to develop, but innovation in that space is now rampant. In 1992, Apple inventor Steve Wozniak launched his first non-Apple venture with Core, a remote control that had the same amount of memory and processing power as the Apple II computer invented just 15 years earlier. Wireless keyboards are now a common accessory for digital televisions with Internet access and other interactive features.

Portable, pocket-sized keyboards for text entry will probably soon be superseded by voice recognition technology. We have already seen the replacement of the computer mouse with touch pads. From yet another angle, wearable computers are being deployed for field technicians or clerks to perform hands-free data collection, and even for transmission of that data over wireless links to central servers.

Extended Capabilities

Other capabilities that have no analog in human organisms, but that have clear utility, are now becoming available. Agent technology, search engines, phone-number portability, robot travelers, smart cars, holographics, smart houses, virtual reality (downloading tactile and eventually cognitive stimulation) are all emerging technologies that will profoundly influence the way we interact with digital media and with each other.

For instance, smart home technology, currently being developed by companies like Cisco, Microsoft, Sun, and others, involves control protocols (NetWorks, JINI, Universal Plug'n'Play) for a range of home features, including home heating, microwave ovens, refrigerators, player pianos, gas fireplaces, window shades, and automobiles.

Nontechnical Infostructure

I spent ten years working in the somewhat surreal culture of inside-the-beltway Washington, D.C., but also living in the very real city of Washington. Most of white-collar, political Washington lives in the suburbs and commutes into the so-called Federal Triangle bounded by the White House, the Capitol, and the Washington monument. I, on the other hand, lived in the city proper, whose population is predominantly Afro-American. Among the many things I learned living as a minority in that environment is that the Afro-American culture is a verbal culture. People are constantly on the phone—even while working—with their sisters, mothers, and friends. This kind of street culture morphs continually and develops as fast as any digital technology. So it is not surprising to me that African Americans were among the first to pick up on digital communication. Pagers and cell phones are often visible in otherwise low-income neighborhoods. Some of these may actually be attributable to the sometimes deliberate and often inaccurate stereotype of drug dealers, but even that fact may be significant of cultural adaptation. Likewise, the innovators of rap music built on their verbal culture and integrated cutting-edge musical engineering technology into their art form.

Author Neal Stephenson, often cited as a thematic relative if not a disciple of William Gibson, wrote in his novel, *The Diamond Age*, of a subculture called the Drummers, who interact primarily through apparently random and promiscuous sexual relations. The Drummers, however, used sexuality as a means to communicate information, including genetic information. I often wonder if Stephenson's Drummers were inspired by modern tribal musical events like rock concerts. One such event, the modern rave, is explicitly recognized as such by its aficionados:

> At the heart of the rave is a modern, technologically-clad form of non-verbal, ecstatic communion. The ethos of openness, sharing, intimacy, touch and empathy—not to mention the pure intensities of trance itself—facilitated by the use of LSD and MDMA in tandem with the all-night-long pulsation of bodies to the same sound source, can and does create a context where layers of armoring and conditioning are shed, where those willing can find the joyful and mysterious realm of their bodies free of oh-so-many enculturated ego-trips and bullshit. . . . A collective molting ritual for the new species.[15]

These other methods of communication, some not so obvious, may still serve the purposes of the neurosphere. Yet no medium has leapt so dramatically onto our collective cultural radar screen as the World Wide Web. And as noted earlier, it is no longer accessed exclusively through the medium of the general-purpose personal computer.

INTERNALIZING THE INTERNET

Walking around my first Consumer Electronics Show in Las Vegas in January 1999, I was struck by the intensity of the digital revolution creating ever smaller, more powerful communication devices—wearable computers, voice-activated units, embedded microchip technology, handheld scanning and translation devices, and more.

At that Consumer Electronics Show, an exhibit called the High-Tech Habitat showed video cameras disguised as hanging artwork or inkpens. This increasing sophistication of high-end video equipment has been accompanied by a corresponding radical drop in digital video equipment prices. Analog televisions took forty years to reach the level of commodity pricing; in the digital realm, that transition took about five years. The rapid spread of digital technology is evident in disposable PCs, and smaller and smaller PC form factors like those called "information appliances." Futurist Paul Saffo notes that cheap sensors in devices were as narrowly distributed in 1998 as microprocessors were in 1978–79.[16] Soon we will see small sensors built into many devices, and a corresponding disappearance of the computer as a mediating device.

The Sony Walkman ushered in the era of portability. Since then, a wide range of devices that let us obtain and manipulate outside data and entertainment sources have become available—handheld scanner pens that translate and define words, wearable computers, PC-based home weather stations, and Global Positioning Satellite receivers built into wristwatches. Moreover, a survey of these products makes clear that there is also a trend afoot toward monitoring, collecting, and manipulating information internal to our bodies— vital signs, blood pressure, and even brainwaves. These devices include home-use prenatal listening devices, personal heart monitors, and handheld CO_2 pollution monitors.

These innovations support the idea that we are becoming increasingly— and almost literally—plugged into each other. PlanetWeb, for instance, is just one of several companies that have developed Web browsers (like Netscape and Internet Explorer) in extremely compact code that can fit in almost any device, no matter how small. So all the capabilities and advantages of the Web described so far can be ported to all manner of portable hardware devices—perhaps even to microdevices implanted in our bodies.

Much of the discussion of computer trends and services in the previous section assumed personal computers as mediating devices that allow individuals to connect to the Internet or interact with other individuals. As Moore's Law has continued its inexorable march, however, ever-increasing computing power has been concentrated in smaller and smaller microprocessors, until that computing power can be built into virtually any device. Miniaturization enables fingertip awareness and control of information that was previously diffused across many individuals and many institutions. This personalized awareness and control may soon be shared across groups—implementing, by definition, a type of group consciousness. An analog of an expanded awareness of the outer world is the growth of conscious awareness of internal states and control of previously autonomous bodily functions, as demonstrated by some of the devices listed above.

When technology mediates between ourselves and the outside world, and between ourselves and our own bodies, this clearly has effects on our consciousness. Further, as individuals, we can select desired effects through our choice of technology. This dynamic is articulated by Steve Mann, a pioneer in the development of wearable computers:

> I have melded technology with my person and achieved a higher state of awareness than would otherwise be possible. I see the world as images imprinted onto my retina by rays of light controlled by several computers, which in turn are controlled by cameras concealed inside my glasses.[17]

> Every morning I decide how I will see the world that day. Sometimes, I give myself eyes in the back of my head. Other days, I add a sixth sense, such as the ability to feel objects at a distance. If I am going to ride my bicycle, I want to feel the cars and trucks pressing against my back, even if they are a few hundred feet away.

Things appear different to me than they do to other people. I see some items as hyperobjects that I can click on and bring to life. I can choose stroboscopic vision to freeze the motion of rotating automobile tires and see how many bolts are on the wheels of a car going over 60 miles per hour, as if it were motionless. I can block out the view of particular objects, sparing me the distraction, for example of the vast sea of advertising around me. I live in a video graphic world,. It is as if my entire life were a television show. Indeed, many people assume that by living my life through the screen, I do exactly what television leads us to do—tune out reality. In fact, WearComp has quite the opposite effect. Visual filters help me concentrate on what is important, heightening my sensitivity and setting my imagination free.[18]

This internalization of computing power is accelerating. It is therefore inevitable that computing power will become integrated directly into human beings and drive physical functioning of everything from the eyes to the legs to the heart. Can the brain be far behind?

The Electric Human

"The Perennial Philosophy . . . the ethic that places Man's final end in the knowledge of the immanent and transcendent Ground of all being. . . . Direct knowledge of the Ground cannot be had except by union."

—ALDOUS HUXLEY

INCREASINGLY, various biotechnology breakthroughs seem to enable incorporation of technology directly into the body, including the brain. The integration of the individual mind with the information and telecommunication infrastructure marks the formation of a tangible neurosphere. This is the full manifestation of the new species *homo electric.*

I was born too late for the "Summer of Love." When I did hit college, however, I took on many of the trappings of the hippie generation that was fast fading from the national scene. One of the more productive attitudes I adopted, besides an outspoken appreciation of peace and love, was a desire to find a greater degree of spiritual fulfillment.

I read the classics of Eastern mysticism, from the *Bhagavad Gita* to the *Tao Te Ching*. I threw the *I Ching* and learned to meditate. I assembled an outlook that, like that of many of my generation, borrowed from many cultures, yet lacked a cohesive structure or any cultural history. For all the flaws in this scattergun approach, it led me, after years of thinking about these matters, to a very strong belief in the potential for self-improvement—improvement, not just in spiritual contentedness, but in day-to-day behavior, health, and physical and mental function.

I began Tai Chi lessons with all the enthusiasm of a true believer, believing that it would be the synthesis of strategies for physical and mental improvement. After a year, however, I had a hard time seeing any real improvement. I began to get impatient as our teacher, who spoke only Chinese, was unable to convey any sense of what improvement I should expect, and how it would look or feel. Toward the end of that first year, my teacher launched a second beginner's class, whose students came in after we finished each week. Around that time, I noticed that we were learning very few new movements, only repeating the old ones. And after a few more months, suddenly that class of beginners joined my class *en masse*. Then the teacher launched yet another beginner's class. I began to perceive that this teacher was not unlike any number of "gurus" who promised enlightenment and delivered only lighter wallets.

I was discouraged, yet never stopped looking for the answers that would unlock human potential. I learned to be satisfied with small, gradual improvements in personal function resulting from diligent exercise or career-development initiatives. And yet something more—something just beyond my reach—always seemed possible. I finally realized that technology was the tool that would help me successfully play the cards I'd been dealt by genetics.

JACKING IN

The term "cyberspace" was coined by visionary novelist William Gibson. His work is more literature than straight technology speculation, but he did further coin a vernacular term for the hardwiring of consciousness into the very stuff of the infosphere that we've been talking about. He called this process "jacking in." If the mind is indeed electrical in nature, he claimed, it is a short step to think about how mind can connect directly to electrical information-storage environments, or directly intervene in electrical control systems, biological function, and the activity of consciousness itself.

The Electrical Nature of the Brain

Discovery of the electrical nature of the brain's function was nearly coeval with the discovery and harnessing of electricity in the 18th century. Today, electroencephalograms are a valuable method of diagnosing and treating neural dysfunctions.

In 1952 at McGill University, Wilder Penfield began a long career of applying electrical stimulation to various parts of the brain to build a rigorous model of the brain's relations to physical and mental functioning. His work was made possible by advances in technology that supported these delicate procedures. Penfield's electrical stimulation caused many different responses and reflexes, even generating memories. This enabled him to construct an extensive map of the human brain. In all his work, however, Penfield never found that electrode stimulation generated what we would consider actions of consciousness like synthesizing or problem solving. Penfield believed this was at least negative evidence that the mind is not accounted for by brain.[1]

These neuroelectric basics were just the point of departure for a range of research demonstrating the role of electricity in the central nervous system. Marcel Just, at the University of Pittsburgh, is using state-of-the-art magnetic resonance imaging scanners to map activity in the brain. This technology detects changes in blood oxygen levels in each cubic millimeter of gray matter. Further advanced neural research has mapped the frequencies of eletromagnetic waves (1–30 Hertz) that the brain emanates.

This mapped neural information can be the means of connection to external silicon computing power and electronic control of various mechanisms. There have already been developments in technology that help the paralyzed to walk, the blind to see, and the deaf to hear. Following the same development path that led from Penfield to Just, these neuroelectric prosthetics are currently "gross stimulations of complex neural fields, but resolution will increase."[2]

Neuroelectric Prosthetics

A range of research toward control of neural fields is underway at the U.S. National Institutes of Health, in the Neural Prosthesis Program of the National Institute of Neurological Disorders and Strokes. Stimulation and control of neural activity is primarily aimed at restoring usage of limbs paralyzed by spinal-cord injuries. The program also spans research in speech and auditory prostheses, bladder and diaphragm prostheses, and cerebellar stimulation.

NIH research focuses on designing transmitters to send electronic messages to properly equipped prosthetic limbs or organs, and designing receivers that enable the individual controllers to get feedback from the limbs on pressure, resistance, and positioning. The feedback instantaneously provides context for the next control transmission. Researchers are working at the level of a single neuron and figuring out how neurons make synaptic contacts with other neurons.

One of the inventions resulting from this work is called the Neurochip:

> The neurons used in the network are harvested from the hippocampus of rat embryos. Once the cells have been separated out by a protein-eating enzyme, each is individually inserted into a well in the silicon chip that is about half the diameter of a human hair. The cell is spherical in shape when it is inserted and is slightly smaller in diameter than the silicon chip well. When it is set in place and fed nutrients, it grows dendrites and an axon that spread out of the well.

In doing so, each neuron remains close to a single recording and stimulating electrode within the well, and also links up with other dendrites and axons attached to other neurons in other nearby wells. According to Michael Maher, one of the coinventors:

> This is pretty much a small brain connected to a computer, so it will be useful in finding out how a neural network develops and what its properties are. It will also be useful for studying chemical reactions at the synapses for weeks at a time. With conventional technology, you can record directly from at most a few neurons for at most a couple of hours.[3]

Another invention of this group, called the Neuroprobe, is designed to be permanently implanted into neural tissues. This research group states its goal bluntly: To connect brains to computers.

> The masters of microfabrication in Prof. Tai's lab have also produced silicon probes designed to hold 15 neurons in a line of wells, like the wells of the Neurochip. The Neuroprobe, part of the Neural Prosthesis Program of the National Institute of Neurological Disorders and Stroke (National Institutes

of Health), is designed to be permanently implanted into neural tissue. When the neurons in the wells send out processes and make synaptic contacts with the host tissue, we will have a specific, long-term connection with the tissue for stimulation and recording studies. We collaborate with Prof. Gyorgy Buzsaki at Rutgers University, who is testing the probes in living rats. In our lab, Steve Potter is using cultured hippocampal slices from neonate rats as the host tissue, so that outgrowth from the probe and synaptic integration with the slice can be monitored non-destructively, over time.[4]

CalTech scientists, in another example of this cutting-edge research, are working at the individual neuron level as well. Their research on membrane excitability explores

the ability of a neuron to respond to, encode and transmit chemical and electrical signals. . . . The molecules that allow this communications system to function are being discovered at a breathtaking pace in the field of molecular neuroscience . . . molecules involved in synaptic transmission, the conversion of sensory information from the world, such as light and odors, into patterns of electrical activity; the control of motor output, and the control of more complex activities, such as thinking and computation.[5]

Researchers recently discovered a cortical area or group of neurons in monkeys and humans that encodes the next intended arm movement. This area may be ideally suited to provide control signals for guiding real or prosthetic arms. The encoding of arm movement in a normal brain and body is read out or interpreted by motor-related cortical areas where the detailed commands for motor action are created. After even further refinement by brainstem and spinal-cord neurons, the control signals eventually activate muscle groups in the arm. This is the signal path that is destroyed by limb injury, which researchers are seeking to replace with artificial electrical pathways. In particular, researchers plan micro-neurosurgical implantation of a silicon electrode array—electrodes that will carry algorithms for translating neural activity into arm-control signals.[6]

Other NIH research grants are funding development of microstimulators and microtransducers for neuromuscular stimulation.

[These microtechnologies] selectively stimulate paralyzed muscles in a controlled fashion to permit an individual to use his or her own muscles as the motors to produce limb movement. Multiple implantable microtransducers

that sense contact, grasping force and position from either implanted trans-
ducers or intact sensory receptors may provide sensory feedback from an
otherwise insensate limb.[7]

The stimulation at first takes place through signals generated from outside
the body, but then migrates to voluntary control generated internally.[8]

Research supported by progress in electrical stimulation for selective activation or inhibition of neurons in the central nervous system using single
penetrating microelectrodes has established safe levels of stimulation.
Resolution continues to increase, matched with development of miniaturized,
closely spaced penetrating microelectrodes.

In addition to developing prosthetic limbs, NIH is funding research in
auditory prosthetics to assist the hearing impaired. One example is a percutaneous (beneath the skin—as opposed to transcutaneous, on top of the skin)
connector system to permit direct connections between signal processors
outside the body and electrode arrays in close proximity to sensory neurons
in the brain. A high-density percutaneous connector allows the flexibility of
direct connections to implanted electrodes in auditory prostheses without the
bandwidth and signal-parameter limitations of transcutaneous connections.
In this example, researchers are also benefiting from state-of-the-art biocom-
patible materials, meaning materials that may be implanted without compli-
cations of infection or immune-system responses.

Neuroelectrical research is also focused on visual prosthetics. Recently, a
blind individual had an array of 38 microelectrodes with percutaneous leads
implanted into her visual cortex for a period of three months. She could see
and describe visual phosphenes produced by electrical stimulation through
the electrodes. Researchers are now seeking permanent implants in concert
with an external sensor device that transmits visual information to the brain.

New Neuroelectric Capabilities

Using technology to repair somatic damage is often cited as one of the won-
derful effects of scientific advance. People seem unsettled by consideration of

how technology may actually give new capabilities, however. That line of thinking is already controversial in the sporting world, where the use of steroids or other artificial "supplements" is generally thought to be "unfair." People are even more unsettled when it comes to supplementing the operation of the brain. This unease is reflected in reactions to developments in neural-network research aimed at better enabling computers to work like human brains—for instance, in chess-playing computers.

Other examples surface every day. IBM's Almaden Research Center invented Personal Area Networks using the natural electrical conductivity of the human body to transmit electronic data. Using a small prototype transmitter with an embedded microchip, two people can transmit messages through a simple handshake. The PAN creates an external electrical field that passes a tiny current through the body over which data is carried. The current is one-billionth of an amp—by comparison, the electrical field generated by running a comb through your hair is 1,000 times greater.

Professor Kevin Warwick, of the University of Reading in Britain, recently had a chip implanted in his body that activates sensors when he enters a room. His first application was a computer voice telling him he had email waiting when he entered his office.[9] A further evolutionary step was demonstrated by Emory University in Georgia, where a device was implanted in a paralyzed man's brain that let him move a cursor across a computer screen using only brain signals.[10]

Most of these examples, however, are just new applications of the "same old brain." Current research encompasses activities such as hippocampal neuron patterning, or actually growing living neurons on computer chips. Essentially, researchers are building brains out of organic materials.[11] It is a short step from there to adding neurons to the human brain to replace those lost to disease or damage, adding raw processing capability (improving my absentmindedness?), adding specific stored knowledge, or adding new capabilities (playing the piano).

This type of research leads us to speculate about whether we are making quantitative changes in brain function, or whether we are closer to answering questions about the difference between the brain and the mind.

The Human Electrical Field

Electrical activity in the brain is well documented. The extension of electrical activity outside the skin is not so well accepted. Yet some research indicates that electrical fields generated by the body and brain may extend outside the body. Such New Age gimmicks as Kirlian photography notwithstanding, it may be possible for individuals to exert some conscious control over these fields. This mechanism could then enable the wireless interconnection of human consciousness with a physical neurosphere.

Dr. Robert Becker and others have mapped electrical fields in the human body—what Becker calls, after poet Walt Whitman, The Body Electric. The electrical pattern of an animal is as real as its cells, skin, and teeth. The fact that acupuncture points are correlated with identifiable electrical patterns is probably not surprising to acupuncturists. At the very least, however, this emerging map of the electric human provides a basis for some interesting investigations.[12]

There is some evidence that external electromagnetic fields may have both positive and negative effects on the human body. Experimenters in Russia have used electrical current to induce sleep. They have also used it to bring the benefit of a full night's sleep to individuals who have slept only two or three hours.

Becker has done extensive work demonstrating that electrical current stimulates the healing rate of the human body. Moreover, electrical fields appear to persist where animal limbs have been severed, and appear to be the mechanism by which animals such as lizards regenerate severed limbs.[13] It is well known that the physical components of the body—skin cells, bones, and blood—are eroded or ejected and replaced constantly. "Over a seven-year period, there is no part of us that is made of the same material that existed seven years earlier."[14]

Other applications of Becker's theories include transcutaneous electrical nerve stimulation (TENS) for pain relief.[15] There also appears to be some evidence that pain can be controlled through conscious control of direct current. This may work either by shutting off pain messages or by sending signals that release endorphins. Becker suggests that biological control systems (how salamander cells know to regrow a hind leg rather than a foreleg) work in a simple negative feedback loop. Becker postulates that "such systems in living organisms would very likely be electric in nature."[16]

On the potentially negative side, electrical currents can also apparently cause cancer-cell growth.[17] The National Institute of Environmental Health Sciences has conducted a survey of the effects of 60 Hertz electromagnetic fields (EMFs) found around high-voltage power transmission lines.[18] Physiological effects reported in some laboratory studies include changes in functions of cells and tissues, decrease in melatonin, alterations of the immune system, accelerated tumor growth, changes in biorhythms, and changes in human brain activity and heart rate.

The NIEHS concludes carefully that the changes reported "may be within the normal variation" and "a biological response to a particular stimulus does not necessarily result in a negative health effect." Further, "ELF-EMF exposure cannot be recognized as entirely safe because of weak scientific evidence that exposure may pose a leukemia hazard. In our opinion, this finding is insufficient to warrant aggressive regulatory concern."[19] Since the cosponsor of the study is the U.S. Department of Energy, which has a vested interest in the basic electrical power infrastructure of the nation, this conclusion may be less than reassuring. At least one epidemiological study in Sweden found the risk of leukemia twice as high for individuals living near power lines. Whether a risk or not, the physiological effect seems real enough.[20]

British biologist Rupert Sheldrake has posited the existence of what he calls morphogenetic fields that play a role in the transmission, in an evolutionary sense, of certain characteristics. This is a "field" in a slightly different sense, but very analogous to the concepts of Becker and others.[21] Likewise, physicist

Arthur Young has speculated that DNA may have a superconductive core and may radiate a shortwave radio signal that coordinates cell growth.[22] Thus, electricity may even play a role in genetics, although this is pure speculation at the moment.

It seems clear, says Shallis, that "electrical signals are the means our bodies use to move information around the organs and limbs, senses and brain to provide the basis for our thought processes." Moreover, he continues, "the electric human being presents an intricate, complex and subtle set of electric potentials that interact with each other and with external fields."[23] Here, we are most concerned with the electrical nature of the brain. As Shallis has noted, electricity colors new metaphors that describe mental activity.[24] We talk about being "tuned in," or connecting with the "vibes" of different people. Well, it may not be just talk.

Brainwave Manipulation

Biofeedback was the prototype for a new generation of mind/machine interfaces that emerged in the 1970s and 1980s. Biofeedback generally has measured a number of elements of physical functioning like skin temperature, heart rate, sweat-gland activity, and brainwave activity. It has then presented the results to patients and simply instructed them to attempt, by concentration, to alter the measurements. Practitioners have seen demonstrable effects in reducing stress, for example, by learning to affect its physical symptoms.[25] Among conditions that have been successfully treated by biofeedback (as reported in medical journals) are migraine and tension headaches, as well as other types of chronic pain, disorders of the digestive system, incontinence, high blood pressure, cardiac arrhythmias, attention deficit disorder, and epilepsy.

Thirty years of work have brought significant improvements in the ability to measure and characterize brainwaves. Lexicor Medical Technology Inc. has developed software that displays complex patterns of brainwave activity. Lexicor claims that mental disorders are characterized by certain brainwave patterns and good mental health by others. Lexicor's technology allows mental-health patients to see their own brainwave patterns and, by meditation or other means, attempt to generate healthy patterns that are rewarded by sound or visual displays on a computer screen.

Lexicor claims that 1,500 psychologists, psychiatrists, and clinicians are currently using this therapy on over 100,000 patients. Clinical categories they assert can be treated with this technology include attention deficit disorders, alcoholism, chemical dependencies, anxiety disorders, disassociation, and compulsive criminal behavior. Not so coincidentally, these categories are characteristic of prison populations. Lexicor is targeting this market with brainwave feedback therapies. Needless to say, in 21st-century America, this is a growth sector.

Another generation of technology emerged in the 1980s called mind machines, which focused on altering the electrical activity of the brain by listening to tapes that emit beats at various rates. Listening to these beats generally causes brainwaves to adjust themselves to the same frequencies, a process called entrainment. Certain types of brainwaves are associated with relaxation, for example, and machines are often used to induce a relaxed state. A variety of natural phenomena have the same effect—for instance, ocean waves. In fact, the entrainment effect may explain why people come away from even crowded, noisy beaches feeling refreshed.

As noted earlier, brainwaves are not understood well enough to reveal much about their correspondence to specific thoughts. Whether the control of brainwaves is direct or indirect, however, begs the question of whether the interplay of internal and external electrical activity is possible. Interest in biofeedback declined in the 1980s, but brain research flourished, and the cost of sensors, wireless components, and computer power has plummeted. There is now a new generation of devices that can read subtle brainwave activity. Mind machines have also been used for pain reduction, and some users actually claim lasting effects manifested as increased IQ measurements.

One such device is the IBVA, or the Interactive Brainwave Visual Analyzer.

Marketing materials describe the IBVA as "[a] system created and refined through 27 years of research."

> The IBVA provides easy real time analysis and intricate interactive biofeedback control of brainwave conditions for professionals as well as the curious. Put simply, the IBVA reads your brainwaves in real time and allows you to use them to trigger images, sounds, other software or almost any electronically addressable device through its MIDI, serial and Expansion Pak features. With the network and modem features of the IBVA, your brainwaves can be analyzed and control equipment from anywhere in the world!

> Design with your mind having some say over what's happening with the computer and controllable devices. The interaction influencing an orchestral composition as you are listening (MIDI signals triggering MIDI sequencers), selecting a movie or movie scene (controlling digital video playback or laserdisc players), creating environments while you dream (triggering MIDI equipment while you sleep with who knows what being played), self care, training, sleep monitoring, stress management, meditation, [Put your ideas here].[26]

AquaThought Foundation has produced a similar product based on research into communication with dolphins.

> AquaThought's multifaceted Immersive Media research seeks to develop near-term technologies for tele-present interaction (and the simulation of interaction) with dolphins, and neuronal feedback cognitive-evoked potential protocols for EEG. Our long-term research goals are the dissolution of boundaries between human and information, and the development of transparent human-machine interface technology.

> [AquaThought's commercial product Cyberfin] is an immersive dolphin encounter simulator which will bring virtual dolphin contact to a massive audience. It will virtually transport the user into an underwater location populated with friendly and inquisitive dolphins. Cyberfin began as a research project in "Tele-presence Interaction" with dolphins. Designed to remotely extend the sensory modalities of its user into an underwater dolphin environment, the simulator platform couples to visual, auditory, and nervous sensory systems. AquaThought has designed this method of operation to verify experimentally that the neurological phenomena found to accompany dolphin interaction are indeed attributable to sensory stimulation during the interaction. Cyberfin has since evolved from a research tool into a LBE (location-based entertainment) attraction, employing state-of-

the-art virtual reality and neurotechnology. The content, dolphin contact, is engaging to men, women, and children of all ages.[27]

We must be careful, however, not to let New Age hucksterism obscure the viability of the technology. Even if it does not fulfill all its claims, the technology may still enable some very interesting human/machine interfaces. Indeed, serious academic research into just that possibility proceeds apace.

Drumming is another form of entrainment. The use of percussion as a driver for trance production is well known in many indigenous cultures, and has been rediscovered in the West as well. We are also entrained by the larger patterns of nature and by planetary and astronomical movements, as we will discuss below.

THE ELECTRICAL NATURE OF HUMAN CONSCIOUSNESS

The brain's control of the body through electrical impulses is well understood. As noted in the previous section, this control is being augmented by computers and by currents generated from outside the body. It stands to reason that similar control of consciousness or the mind is also possible through directed electromagnetic stimulation.

Neurobiologist Michael Persinger of McGill University has been prolific in publishing papers on the effects of electromagnetic fields on an extraordinary range of animal and human biological, neurological, and psychological functions. In dozens of articles on topics ranging from geomagnetic activity as a partial parturitional trigger to the effects of enhanced geomagnetic activity on hypothermia, to the possible relationship between geomagnetic activity and epileptic seizures, to associations between sudden infant death syndrome and increments of global geomagnetic activity, Persinger has reported on research whose scope and significance is substantial.[28]

In his most adventurous and controversial work, Persinger and colleagues at McGill's Neuroscience Research Group have applied very weak but complex magnetic fields transcerebrally (across brain hemispheres). The individuals thus exposed experienced a sense of a nearby presence. One of Persinger's objectives is to develop clinical applications to treat abnormal psychology. He believes that reports of UFO contact and similar experiences may be a result of internal or external factors that trigger this sense. Through his research, he seeks ways to control or eliminate such neurological responses. He even extends his theories to mystical religious experiences, which, in his view, are the result of stimulation of what he calls a "God module" in the brain.

Persinger portrays himself as the ultimate reductionist—all experience, he claims, is rooted in simple organic activity. I happen to believe he's doing more to expose the range of impact of electrical activity in the brain and human behavior. Once more, whether the so-called higher functions of consciousness are the result of electricity begs the question of whether humans can control their experience through electrical means.

The Human Brain as Tuner

If consciousness is electrical—or more broadly, electromagnetic—then it may also be useful to define consciousness as a signal. That is, consciousness may be transmitted or received like any other signal occupying a portion of the electromagnetic spectrum. Indeed, philosophers have long struggled with defining consciousness, and with determining whether the mind is distinct from the brain.

The prevailing view, that mind is an emergent property of sufficient neural complexity, stands in contrast to that of earlier thinkers like Plato, William James, and Henri Bergson. They believed that the brain does not produce consciousness, but rather detects, transmits, and filters it.[29] In the last century, pioneer British physicist Sir William Crookes (discoverer of the element thallium) proposed a model of the brain as mental radio. The brain, he claimed, picks up broadcasts from the "soul" (leaving aside the religious connotations of the word) either internal or external to the individual.

Evidence for this model may be accumulating from two directions—the frontiers of quantum physics and the wilderness of psychic phenomena. And as more than one scientist has been forced to conclude, many psychic phenomena have yet to be contradicted by the best current theories of physics.

Consciousness at the Quantum Level

Physicist Nick Herbert directly addresses the intersection of physics and consciousness in his book *Elemental Mind*. In his view, consciousness exists in some form, even at the subatomic level. Consciousness is native to the building blocks of the brain, rather than a by-product of it.

Many physicists, like David Bohm with his implicate order, have talked about the undivided wholeness of the quantum world. In 1964, Bell's theorem proved that nonlocality was consistent with quantum theory (and still is). In other words, any two particles that were once in contact are still in communication in some fashion, no matter how widely separated they have become.[30] Bell's conclusion requires that the world be filled with innumerable nonlocal influences in order to work as it does. Since Bell's formulation, certain experiments seem to suggest that separate human minds are connected in ways considered impossible under mechanistic, physiological models of consciousness.[31]

Sir John Eccles, Nobel Prize winner in Medicine and Physiology, has proposed a role for quantum physics in consciousness based on the way neurotransmitter chemicals seem to be released into the synaptic gap.

> In the human cortex, a rather large number of synapses, perhaps as many as one hundred million, respond on a probabilistic basis to neural excitations. When electrically excited by a nerve impulse, neurons may or may not release a single chemical packet . . . these packets are so small that quantum uncertainty rather than classical thermal agitation governs their release or retention . . . thus, human awareness is a quantum effect.[32]

The synapse acts as a sensitive receiver affected by quantum-level activity rather than chemical reaction. Physicist Evan Walker posits a "second nervous system" connecting distant synapses through quantum-level communication. Tying back to the emergent model, this activity requires some critical mass of conventional nervous activity in the brain before it is activated.

Likewise, English mathematician C.J.S. Clarke published a paper summarized in the following abstract:

> The dominance in normal awareness of visual percepts, which are linked to space, obscures the fact that most thoughts are non-spatial. It is argued that the mind is intrinsically non-spatial, though in perception can become compresent with spatial things derived from outside the mind. The assumption that the brain is entirely spatial is also challenged, on the grounds that there is a perfectly good place for the non-spatial in physics. A quantum logic approach to physics, which takes non-locality as its starting point, offers a nonreductive way of reconciling the experience of mind with the world description of physics. For further progress it is necessary to place mind first as the key aspect of the universe.[33]

The existence of consciousness in some form all the way down to the subatomic level echoes the thought of Teilhard himself. The notion of elemental mind is exactly parallel to Teilhard's conception of the "interiority" of things.

The work of one respected physicist provides a handy transition to the not-so-respected, but philosophically compatible, world of parapsychology. At the Princeton Engineering Anomalies Research Lab, Robert Jahn and Brenda Dunne have shown remote human ability to alter the function of random number generators in replicable, statistically significant experiments. Jahn and Dunne's theory is consistent with the findings of the physicists cited above, in that "the mode of effect is at the micro level, since that is the scale of computer activity." Their conclusions are that "human consciousness is able to extract information from physical aspects of its environment, by some anomalous means that is independent of space and time." Human consciousness, they claim, "is capable of inserting information, in its most rudimentary objective form, namely binary bits, into random physical systems, by some anomalous means that is independent of space and time."[34]

ANOMALOUS HUMAN ELECTRICAL PHENOMENA

It is clear to me that there is more to reality than scientists are willing to admit. And while no one wants to be viewed as a crackpot, the character of the nonordinary (to use the term of the discredited Carlos Castaneda) events in my life and those on the borderline in science all seem to point to the electrical or electromagnetic model described above.

Evolution, as we know it, is punctuated by discontinuities. Missing links persist in the fossil record, because transition periods are so short relative to the longer time scale of species evolution. Phenomena occurring today—things we consign derisively to the realm of the paranormal—may instead be imperfectly understood. They may be totally logical events that will, with the help of more inclusive models of scientific understanding, be seen as the by-products of a transition to a new mode of collective, electrical consciousness. It is, at the very least, instructive to study the literature of anomalous phenomena for hints of future human concerns and, possibly, future human behavior and capabilities.

Human-potential impresario Michael Murphy has attempted to put such beliefs in an empirical frame. After years of hosting a variety of therapists seeking to expand human potential at the Esalen Institute, Murphy compiled the evidence for enhanced human functioning across a range of abilities.[35] The evidence he presents occurs across cultures and across individual differences, and so is presumed latent in all humans. Some of these abilities, like yoga, are due to discipline or study. Others arise spontaneously; some are not even desired by the individuals having the experience. A football player sometimes "sees" the game from a perspective above the field. Yoga practitioners can slow their breathing to extraordinarily low levels. Twins and close family members can establish a telepathic rapport. Christian mystics in some desert orders have demonstrated the ability to endure environmental extremes. Mikhail Baryshnikov and Michael Jordan appear to have an ability to move their bodies in supranormal ways. There are reports of highly focused athletes or fans moving balls through telekinesis. Women use the Lamaze method of birthing to transform pain into happiness. Scientists experience breakthrough insights in moments of contemplation. Biofeedback training claims to enable a permanent lowering of blood pressure. These are all examples of individuals appearing to transcend acknowledged human limits.[36]

Silent Radio

I always accept handbills that are handed to me on the streets of the city. One day, on the corner of Connecticut and K Streets in Washington, D.C., a few blocks from FCC headquarters and a number of very wealthy law firms making tons of money representing telecommunication interests, a gentleman handed me an 8½ x 11 sheet filled with a typed, single-spaced, marginless rant about the FCC's failure to alleviate his problem: messages were being beamed into his head by some unknown party or parties.

I told this to a Washington attorney friend of mine, who told me about his stint at the FCC, where he and his colleagues occasionally received formal complaints about such messages. Jokingly, he referred to the complaints as the responsibility of the Silent Radio Bureau (the FCC being separated into bureaus—Mass Media Bureau, Cable TV Services Bureau, etc.). A humorous response to an apparently humorous situation.

Not all incidents of this kind are humorous, however. Take, for instance, the time that I was doing research that required calls to the general managers of cable television systems around the country. I got the names from a directory notorious for being out of date. I called a place in Minnesota and asked for John Smith. A woman responded in a shaky voice that Mr. Smith was dead. He had been gunned down recently by a man who felt his cable converter box was beaming messages into his head and driving him crazy. Likewise, I once heard a cab driver complain, in an online conferencing service, that his customers were repeating back to him thoughts he had posted on the service, although they were unlikely to have gotten them from this source. He attributed it to a campaign by the religious right to intimidate him so that his influential voice (he was, after all, a cab driver) would be silenced.

While these episodes may invite ridicule, some mental health professionals have remarked on the sometimes-telepathic nature of institutionalized schizophrenics. In the context of Murphy's *Future of the Body*, I often wonder if these poor unfortunates are harbingers of a latent ability in all of us, who are driven mad by their inability to understand their experiences or interpret the input of their own extended senses.

Electrical Sensitives

There is substantial evidence that humans do, indeed, interact with the electrical world around them. Author Michael Shallis coined the term "electrical sensitives" to describe this phenomenon.[37] For example, electrical sensitives get shocks from switches that are functioning normally and that don't affect anyone else. They appear to have an effect on computers and report more problems with their personal computers crashing. They are more likely to receive shocks from appliances and to build up static electricity. Their homes are more likely to be struck by lightning, and they experience increased allergic responses to electricity.

People who live in, or who frequent, areas with ambient electrical fields—like those caused by power lines—often report adverse effects like headaches, nausea, lack of energy, or weakened immune systems. Electrical sensitives, however, have also noted positive effects from certain electrical stimuli. Air ionizers that produce negative charges in the air appear to mitigate the buildup of positive charges inside them.[38] Researcher Leslie Hawkins has conducted studies showing that exposure to negative ions, such as those generated by waterfalls or rushing water, gives individuals a greater feeling of well-being.[39] Likewise, the application of magnetic fields has been shown to aid bone healing.[40]

Shallis tells of a man in Belgium who has "the ability to extinguish street lights, but not on demand. He notices that the occurrence takes place when he is in a particularly distracted and 'distant state of mind.'"[41] A British group called the Association for the Scientific Study of Anomalous Phenomena has collected a casebook of instances of what it calls Street Lamp Interference, or SLI, including reports from seventy-five people who claim to have noticed that street lamps frequently blink off or permanently burn out in their presence, and that this effect persists over months or years. The group's report, however, was supported only by anecdotal evidence; no testing has been done.[42]

Not surprisingly, I also came across a similar report on the Well:

> I don't know what else to call it, but some people seem to have a field generated around them that causes improbable things to occur. I have such a field, and it has caused unbelievable events to occur with a regularity that boggles the mind. . . . Electronic equipment behaves weird sometimes around me. Things happen that go against logic or reason. . . . Perfectly healthy equipment will suddenly behave in the strangest manner. The effect works both ways. Either something really unlikely will go wrong, or a completely hosed system will just start working. . . . By far the most bizarre stuff involves software and computer systems. Just my presence seems at times to alter the normal function of a system . . . email, networks, plug-ins, updates utilities hard drives, even printers and scanners all seem to be influenced.[43]

As much credence as I give to some reports of the paranormal, I always put SLI in the same category as crop circles or past-life regression—just a little too improbable for me. And then, in 1998, I saw the case book that confirmed an experience I had actually had some eight years earlier.

One winter, I noticed on several occasions that street lights went out over my head as I either walked or drove beneath them. I started recording the dates of these events as they got more frequent. After about five months, the occurrences became less frequent. Only in retrospect did I notice that the events peaked in frequency in mid-March, the time at which I learned one of my best friends had been murdered. The street-light phenomenon happened simultaneously with perhaps the worst thing that had ever happened to me. This invested the whole thing with a greater emotional significance. I'm not sure that this precludes the events being coincidental, but it is a truism of occult and paranormal phenomena that strong emotional turmoil is associated with inexplicable events. Adding an improbable precognitive element to my experience may not help to convince me, but it cannot be discounted.

Temporal-lobe Epilepsy

A headline in 1997 read: "Study Suggests Brain May Affect Religious Response." The report ran as follows:

> No one knows why humanity felt its first religious stirrings, but researchers at UC San Diego reported Tuesday that the human brain may be hard-wired to hear the voice of heaven, in what researchers said was the first effort to directly address the neural basis of religious expression.[44]

McGill University researcher Michael Persinger has associated such experiences with a condition called temporal-lobe epilepsy, identified by neurologists as seizures affecting the temporal lobe of the brain. Epilepsy is an electrical disorder. Some people appear to have no risk of seizure unless exposed to flickering lights, disco strobes, or other electrical signals that just happen to be in rhythm with their brain's electrical frequency. The harmonics created by the external signals result in a seizure.[45] The following comments on the condition by writer Paul Devereux are interesting:

> [T]he temporal lobe cortex integrates several sense modes, and is involved with language. Unlike other parts of the brain, the temporal cortex can be rendered electrically unstable or sensitive for prolonged periods, and if sufficiently large parts of the cortex are so effected it is recordable on EEG readings. Beneath the temporal cortex are two connected structures, the hippocampus and the amygdala. Alterations in the function of the hippocampus can change or modify memory and release dreams in the waking state. The amygdala is associated with emotional feelings. Temporal lobe epilepsy occurs because of the chronic occurrence of tiny electrical seizures within the temporal cortex.
>
> [D]ream states, the hearing of voices, the seeing of apparitions and the feeling of compulsions . . . [clinical] stimulation of the hippocampus and amygdala procure identical experiences—alterations in time and space, OBEs, messages may be heard that seem to come from the subjects' environment. Further, ingesting of certain drugs, exposure to electromagnetic fields, other ways to stimulate occurrence of electrical disturbance within temporal tissues can be learned, and techniques have been developed to promote what

we now identify as temporal lobe effects, allowing ESP and mystical experiences to occur.[46]

Combine these observations with our human sensitivity to negative ions or other environmental factors, and we can begin to understand why, for example, ancient ceremonial sites like Stonehenge are located near areas of greater geomagnetic or seismic activity.

Love is Electric

Electricity is now a common metaphor in literature: "[T]he connection between us was immediate and electric." Indeed, the metaphor was used by writers almost as early as electricity itself was harnessed, as in this example from the 1850s:

> [His] gallantry which sent such a strange thrill to her heart as she had not felt since the day she tried the galvanic battery in the Natural Philosophy class at boarding-school.[47]

Perhaps "electrical sensitives" are imagining things. Certainly physicists will tell you that love is not a force of nature. What little research has been performed to date indicates, however, that electrical sensitives are not imagining things at all. Like Michael Murphy, then, we are justified in viewing these human/electric interactions as the beginning of a transformation of human capability. Enhanced abilities are part of a "developmental continuum" encompassing animal, current human, and advanced human capabilities. As an example, consider the following progression:

A frog's dim perception of light

Normal human vision

Enhanced human vision produced by sensory training

Apprehension of extraordinary color and vibrancy reported by religious contemplatives

Murphy speculates that:

> just as the thinnest part of evidence for evolution is absence of transitions
> from the fossil record, growth in human abilities seem to be punctuated in
> the same way. There is evidence around for an evolutionary transformation
> happening now, but it is difficult to put together a comprehensive descrip-
> tion in physics, biology or social science.[48]

I propose that human/electrical interaction, whether the result of evolution
or medical intervention, is well on its way to developing into a more common
human capability. Moreover, just as Murphy has demonstrated that integral
practices exist to enhance each of his categories of increased human functioning, so there may be ways to cultivate and develop these direct human/elec-
trical connections.

THE ELECTRICAL NATURE
OF THE PLANET

Human-electrical interaction takes place in the context of a world that is electromagnetic. Since time immemorial, humans watched lightning with a mix-
ture of fear and awe. At least since Ben Franklin, we have begun to look deeper into nature and have discovered that electricity is fundamental to the world
around us. It should not be surprising that the mechanism of the neurosphere
is electrical in nature.

The U.S. National Oceanic and Atmosphere Administration tells us that
lightning originates around 15,000 to 25,000 feet above sea level when rain-
drops are carried upward until some of them convert to ice. Then, in a sin-
gularly unscientific way, they add:

> For reasons that are not widely agreed upon, a cloud-to-ground lightning
> flash originates in this mixed water and ice region. The charge then moves
> downward in 50-yard sections called step leaders. It keeps moving toward
> the ground in these steps and produces a channel along which charge is
> deposited. Eventually, it encounters something on the ground that is a good
> connection. The circuit is complete at that time, and the charge is lowered
> from cloud to ground.[49]

Thus, although the conditions for its existence are known, the precipitating cause of lightning remains a mystery.

The Ground below Us

If you look at the fundamental structure of the universe as represented in the periodic table of elements, the whole infinite variety of matter and energy is composed of the difference in the number of electrons in any given atom. As physicist Szent-Gyorgy put it:

> Matter was primarily electrical and materials acquired their different structural characteristics from the shaping effect of electric fields. . . . [L]ife is the property of large molecules to interact and react because of their special electronic characteristics.[50]

Planets with liquid cores, like the Earth, have magnetospheres.[51] It has been shown that the presence of underground water inside a rotating sphere also creates electromagnetic fields. This may explain how, for example, a phenomenon like dowsing works.

The fluid nature of the Earth's interior also inspires other theories. Tectonic pressures preceding earthquakes likely generate an electrical field. Folk wisdom holds that animals exhibit excitement prior to earthquakes. At least one study has demonstrated a sensitivity in animals to changes in environmental electrical fields, and this may be one mechanism that explains that behavior.[52] Electrical fields also generate light and heat, and at least one researcher has found that unexplained lights or UFOs statistically correlate with known earthquake fault zones in the United States.[53] We will further explore the attribution of meaning to apparent electrical environmental influences and internal electrical environmental influences like temporal-lobe epilepsy in chapter 5.

The Sky above Us

Many people seek out a perch next to a waterfall as an especially restful place to commune with nature. Some report that such places leave them feeling not only refreshed, but more alert. Crashing waves and waterfalls generate an excess of negative ions, and ambient levels of electrical activity may be the source of that perceived well-being.

Researchers Krueger and Reed found that "small air ions are biologically active."[54] Preliminary research shows that airborne ions can have "a pervasive effect on the concentration of serotonin."[55] Serotonin, in turn, increases electrical firing in the brain, giving a greater feeling of well-being.[56] Mice and rats display a charge-related metabolic response to air ions, and ion deprivation increases the cumulative mortality rate among mice infected with influenza.

I live in Colorado, where it is axiomatic that "life is better." The Colorado Plateau (the so-called Four Corners region, where the borders of Colorado, Utah, New Mexico, and Arizona meet) is a roughly 350-mile-diameter circle of tangential fault lines. The same area contains the greatest number of high mountain peaks in North America outside of Alaska. The landbase also supports the San Juan Basin uranium field, coal reserves, and an extensive cave system. These four geologic features (faults, mountain peaks, radioactive minerals, and caves) are all components of land-associated atmospheric ionization processes—i.e., stripping air molecules of electrons that can give the air an electric charge. The Four Corners area is also known for having the highest incidence of lightning in North America.[57] There is "probably some electrical anomaly that attracts electric discharges from the sky," Shallis notes. It is well known that lightning strikes some places more often than others, indicating that lightning is not a random process.[58]

In the same vein, mountaintops are well known throughout human history as places of divine and ecstatic visions. The tops of mountains receive ions swept up by prevailing winds, and hence are highly charged. Visionary experience may then be triggered by this condition. (Michael Persinger and Paul Devereux would surely agree.)

Psychologists have noted the influence of negative and positive ions on mood, linking serotonin levels to the effects of SRI drugs like Prozac, Seroxat, and other contemporary mood-altering drugs.[59] On the negative side, Robert

Becker claims a significant relationship between the rate of hospital admissions for people with schizophrenia and manic-depressive psychosis and the occurrence of major magnetic storms in the atmosphere.[60] It is also worth noting in this context that we are at a heightened stage in the Sun's regular cycle of electrical activity. Solar storms that bombard the Earth with highly-charged, ionized particles have disrupted communication systems and even caused electrical blackouts. In the light of these striking physical effects, the apparent effects on humans should not be considered extraordinary.

Electric Animals

Humans are not the only species affected by electricity. Harold Burr, Professor of Anatomy at Yale, studied the correspondence of electric fields with trees, air, and the Earth. Acknowledging that we are bathed in a constant stream of solar electromagnetic radiation, Burr made some basic comparisons and found that the increased electromagnetic output from the Sun during sunspot cycles showed up in tree rings.[61] He also found, in research on living moulds, that "the veins or directions in which the protoplasm flowed were governed by the direction of the electrical field. By altering that field, by changing the electrical environment in which the mould lived, the direction of motion and growth of the slime mould could be altered."[62]

A recent news item noted that:

> [F]ire ants in Texas like living in and eating electrical equipment. . . . They have some short-range attraction to electricity, become mesmerized, and they signal to other members of their communities to join them.[63]

Lewis Thomas observes, in an ironic comment, that "[I]f we were ever to put all our brains together in fact, to make a common mind the way the ants do, it would be an unthinkable thought, way over our heads."[64]

Likewise there are species of fish that actually generate and use electricity.

> Electric fish are able to hunt and navigate without vision, using electric organs to generate electric fields around their bodies to sense where things are. For example, brown ghost knife fish live in the Amazon river and have an electric generating organ in their tails producing a continuous electrical

signal. The signal propagates through the muddy Amazon water and reflects off of objects in the fish's environment. Receptors on the skin sense disturbances in the electrical flow, with different types of objects generating different reflections.[65]

These fish use the same electrical organ for communicating with each other. Moreover, some electric fish can rapidly regenerate lost body parts, recalling the work of Becker discussed earlier.[66] "Electric fish can generate quite strong potentials that can deliver a shock that humans can feel."[67]

The study of electric fish also yields another possible pathway to neuroelectric prosthetics. Scientist Freeman Dyson writes:

> Radioneurology might take advantage of electric and magnetic organs that already exist in many species of eels, fish, birds and magnetotactic bacteria. In order to implant an array of tiny transmitters into a brain, genetic engineering of existing biological structures might be an easier route than microsurgery.[68]

Big Electric Cats

Both respected and somewhat marginalized thinkers have tried to discern meaning in their observations of the electrical nature of the planet and man's place in it. Nicola Tesla was a genius whose discoveries form the backbone of the electric utilities we all use today. Many of Tesla's inventions stemmed from his perceptions of the electrical nature of the world, which he perceived as

> [An] infinitesimal world, with the molecules and their atoms spinning and moving in orbits, carrying with them static charges. . . . The spinning of the molecules and their ether sets up the ether tensions or electrostatic strains; the equalization of ether tensions sets up other motions or electric currents, and the orbital movements produce the effects of electro- and permanent magnetism.[69]

Tesla did not just harness electricity to be delivered over wires. He foresaw other developments:

> We shall have no need to transmit power at all [someday] . . . our machinery will be driven by a power obtainable at any point of the universe. Such is the [meaning of the] myth of Antheus, who derives power from the Earth . . . throughout space there is energy . . . it is a mere question of time when

men will succeed in attaching their machinery to the very wheelwork of nature.[70]

Tesla partially proved these ideas with his wireless lamps—electrodeless discharge lamps inductively coupled to a high-frequency power supply. He invented these lamps after discovering that gases at reduced pressure exhibit extremely high conductivity. The lamps could be moved anywhere in a room with no wired connection, yet they would—eerily—continue to burn. The secret behind these lamps is still being investigated today if patent applications are any indication.[71] Conspiracy theorists, of course, believe that Tesla was silenced by Edison and others for talking about essentially "free" energy.

Not surprisingly, Tesla was a firm believer in "cold fire," a form of electrical therapy for "refreshing the mind" that he applied to himself.[72] This therapy drew on a principle related to the negative ion effect discussed earlier. On the down side, during several nervous breakdowns, Tesla's perceptions became so acute that "[he] could hear a watch ticking three rooms away. A fly landing on a table in his room caused a dull thud in his ear."[73]

Tesla's ultimate, unproven, claim was that he could harness electrical energy to split the Earth. Outlandish as that sounds, Tesla did note that the Earth itself "resonates" at frequencies of 8, 14, and 20 Hertz. In some experiments, Tesla was able to build up large amounts of energy by amplifying lower energy sources through resonance. Though he left this work unfinished, others continue to investigate resonance phenomena.

Another pioneer relegated to the fringe is the psychologist Wilhelm Reich, who split from his mentor Freud and attempted to outline the physical underpinning of human psychology. Among his theories, Reich proposed that an otherwise unseen, unmeasurable bioelectric energy exists within the human being. This energy is constrained and congested by psychic traumas and will inhibit psychotherapy unless integrated with treatment of these physical problems. He called this phenomena "character armor." The same bioelectric energy, he claimed, was present in the atmosphere, and this he called *orgone*.[74] While bioelectric energy is related to electromagnetic energy, he pointed out, it is more subtle and "moves extremely slowly."

Reich invented an orgone accumulator—a box that supposedly captured this subtle energy—in which an individual could lie to restore this bioelectric energy. Celebrities like actor Orson Bean endorsed the therapy in the 1950s. Scientific authorities did not and, amazingly, had Reich put in prison because of his unconventional theories, even burning his books. He died in prison (again, conspiracy theorists take note). Nevertheless, influential founders of popular third-force psychological therapies that integrate physical therapy traced their origins to Reich's theories. Rolfing is an example.

Physicist Itzhak Bentov looks at electromagnetism in the world and within individuals as vibrations. In his book, *Stalking the Wild Pendulum*, he wrote:

> We are made up of vibrations—these affect the environment, and the vibrations of the environment are picked up by our senses. . . . Reality is made up of mostly empty space filled with oscillating fields. If the underlying reality is vibration, then there is an obvious possibility of interconnection and communication or control between the individual and the larger fields of the world—in Bentov's view, the neurosphere is the "unified field of consciousness and planet."[75]

Bentov believes, as do Teilhard and physicist Herbert, that all matter has consciousness: "We usually only recognize a certain level of organization of matter to have consciousness," he explains. "[But] matter is actually a vibrating component of consciousness, as are we." The physical body, then, is an instrument that allows us to interact best with our physical environment. One mechanism for consciously tuning into the larger field of the neurosphere is meditation.

> The body is interpenetrated by bodies or fields having higher vibratory rates—sometimes some of us can tune them in. . . . The resonant frequency of the Earth is 7.5 cycles per second. [7.5 Hertz] . . . the micromotion of the body is 6.8–7.5 Hertz. This suggests a tuned resonant system. . . . We may say now that in deep meditation, the human and the planet start resonating and transferring energy. This occurs at a very long wavelength of about 40,000 km, or just about the perimeter of the planet. Such a long wavelength knows no obstacles and does not attenuate much over long distances.[76]

Not so incidentally, if you think back to the discussion of non-locality, this kind of interpenetrated system means the individual is "local" everywhere in the neurosphere.

Art historian Jose Arguelles is the infamous founder of the Harmonic Convergence. His book, *Earth Ascending*, presents the scientific basis of his millennial theories, which are reminiscent of other, less ambitious, theories of the intersection of biology and electricity. Arguelles notes that the whole Earth generates a standing wave of 6.⁴ Hertz—the same as the human *theta* brainwave associated with deep levels of meditation. The core of Arguelles' thought is what he calls the resonant field model, which views the universe as we know it as the interplay of electromagnetic, gravitational, and "biopsychic" fields. He observes that the following social evolution of man follows the same pattern around the world:

1. Aboriginal

2. Hieratic (empires)

3. Medieval

4. Industrial

He attributes that commonality to the same resonant field acting on humans everywhere and bases parts of his musings on the theories of physicist Oliver Reiser. It was Reiser who posited the Van Allen radiation belts as a "conscious" planetary membrane, corresponding to Teilhard's "super-active film." The two belts of heavy protons and a lighter electron outer belt serve, not only as a radiation shield, but also as an "electromagnetic membrane recharging and recirculating the atmosphere of the Earth."[77]

Arguelles now says that all evidence indicates that we are at the stage of the "hominisation" (a term that Teilhard also used) of the planet. Arguelles coined the term "radiosonic" to describe the "sensory fusion" of the senses and technology. He felt that psychic activity was a real and natural outgrowth of a holistic and interpenetrated world. This recurring theme among scientific and visionary thinkers (and maybe crackpots) should by now be evident. It is a theme that I find compelling.

THE PORTABLE MIND

Taken a step further, the electrical nature of consciousness suggests an affinity to computer equipment that extends beyond the interfaces that mind directly controls. On the other side of the interface lie machines controlled by electronic brains, blurring the distinction between our mind on one side of the interface and the machine's on the other. If the human mind is an electrical field, it may exist apart from the brain, or the specific organic "hardware" that generated it. Individual consciousness may disappear if the brain that spawned it goes away, unless that brain is replaced by other kinds of hardware. Such musings have spawned a whole speculative field of endeavor dubbed "transhumanism."

Moreover, the very existence of the mind as a field—or, put another way, as information—suggests another metaphor of mind as software. Software, as we know from the computer industry, is constantly ported from one hardware platform to another. If the brain is one "hardware" platform (writer Rudy Rucker coined the term "wetware"), then the mind may be transported to other hardware platforms, silicon-based or otherwise.

I use the term "mind" interchangeably with "soul" or "spirit" because I think that is where much of theology leads, absent any specific denominational dogma. In the context of this book, I call this supraphysical entity an "identifield"—that part of the human that transcends the body and contains the kernel of self-consciousness that is essential to what makes us human.

The concept of an identifield can be traced back to ancient times. Many religions have posited the existence of a soul or spirit. Early terms for these concepts usually relate to the root *pneuma*, or breath. Breath, of course, was the observed difference between a living and dead human. The breath was simply abstracted as the vitalizing force within each person. The idea of a soul is an article of faith for millions, perhaps billions, even today. However, a few free thinkers (or heretics) have been trying to operationalize the identifield in nonreligious terms.

Occultist George Gurdjieff, for example, said that there is such a thing as a soul, but we aren't born with it. It's innate, but has to be developed. If we do that well enough—through mental, emotional, and physical exercises— the identifield will survive the end of the biological mechanism without need for blind faith.

Out-of-Body Experiences

Once you accept the existence of a soul or "identifield," it is but a brief step to propose that the soul can leave the body, since it is not identical with it. Some Eastern religions posit "astral travel" as an ability resulting from years of rigorous exercises in yogic control of the body and mind. Robert Monroe, a former cable television executive, claimed to have had such experiences. He attempted to take them out of the occult realm through a book, *Journeys Out of the Body*, which catalogued his own spontaneous out-of-body experiences (usually abbreviated as OBE). Monroe even proposed exercises for eliciting such experiences. The Monroe Institute, after twenty years, still does a thriving business in training sessions, tapes, and publications.

Psychiatrist Stanislav Grof performed extensive research with LSD in Czechoslovakia when "acid" was still legal (and Czechoslovakia was still a country). Grof conducted a study of several hundred LSD sessions and found the following consistent framework in his patients' experiences:

Aesthetic experiences like a greater appreciation of classical music.

Psychodynamic systems in which past experiences with the same theme and emotional quality combine into a system influencing current behavior.

Perinatal memories, one of which is an oceanic, blissful union with one's mother in the womb.

Transpersonal experiences, which are classic examples of expanded consciousness in which the mind moves beyond the body. One consistent positive benefit of transpersonal experiences for Grof's patients was a tendency to incorporate a spiritual dimension into their way of life.

Grof and others formed the Association for Transpersonal Psychology, which publishes a journal that explores these states of consciousness. Another member of the Association—the aforementioned Charles Tart, pioneer psychologist who studied LSD's effects—coined the term "altered states" to describe these experiences. Tart felt that subjective states of consciousness can be identified consistently and compared to the subjective experience of others, so that we have consensus descriptions of other states. Presumably, we can then devise techniques for entering those specific states in a replicable fashion and attain knowledge of what specific states can be used to do or see. Transpersonal experience thus becomes a subset of experience that can be replicated and studied scientifically.

The prohibition of LSD removed a key research tool for achieving these altered states of consciousness in a reliable way. However, the seminal research of the 1950s and early 1960s spawned a sophisticated theory of transpersonal states, which tends to corroborate the discussion here, although from a different perspective.

Sensory deprivation or flotation tanks were also used to precipitate these altered states. Tanks were a minor craze in the 1970s, made infamous by the movie *Altered States*. Long before that movie, however, I had found the experience of floating in a totally dark and silent environment a highly relaxing one. One exercise recommended by tank inventor John Lilly involves moving your sense of self—which most of us locate in our heads—around your body. Several times, I found that "moving" my mind down into my chest area increased the volume of the sound of my own pulse. Moving my mind lower into my stomach area elicited sounds of my stomach gurgling. It is hard to convey to others the sense that this was not an exercise of imagination, but rather my senses, without external inputs, becoming attuned to internal inputs. Again, yoga practitioners confirm the reality and replicability of this kind of experience.

Pigs in Cyberspace

Pioneer cyberneticist Norbert Wiener, who coined the term "cybernetic" from whence all cyber-terminology has flowed, said that some machines are precisely analogous to human functioning in their attempts to control entropy through feedback. Wiener claimed that "the physical functioning of the living individual and the operation of some of the newer communication machines are precisely parallel in their analogous attempts to control entropy through feedback."[78] Likewise, mathematician and author Rudy Rucker characterizes current work on artificial intelligence as an extension of the basic theme of computers—i.e., that they model the human brain. If the programming art were sufficiently extended and deepened, he claims, we could, theoretically, reproduce anyone's mind as a complex software pattern, store it on a chip, and place it in whatever vehicle that person desired.

Perhaps the foremost scientific proponent of downloading the mind is Carnegie-Mellon University engineering professor Hans Moravec. In an essay called "Pigs in Space", Moravec wrote:

> As [the brain] begins to malfunction, might we not choose to use the same advanced neurological electronics that make possible our links to the external world, to replace the gray matter as it begins to fail? Bit by bit, our brain is replaced by electronic equivalents, which work at least as well, leaving our personality and thoughts clearer than ever. Eventually everything has been replaced. . . . No physical vestige of our original body or brain remains, but our thoughts and awareness continue. . . . We will call this process the downloading of a human mind into a machine.[79]

Computers like IBM's chess-playing Deep Blue already outperform human brains at special purpose tasks:

> Generality is an almost magical property, but it has costs. A general purpose machine may use ten times the resources as one specialized for a task. But if the task should change, as it usually does in research, the general machine can simply be reprogrammed, while the specialized machine must be replaced.[80]

Thus Moravec and others have begun to make gross calculations of just how powerful computer hardware would have to be to fully replicate the human brain or host the mental complexity of a human. Moravec extrapolated from the computer brain needed to process data from the human retina and estimated that the entire functioning of a brain could be approximated by a computer performing 10 trillion calculations per second, or 10 teraflops.[81] Given current trends in the cost of computing power, 10 teraflops could be available in a $10 million supercomputer before 2010, and in a personal computer by 2030.[82]

A first tentative step toward validating transhuman theories was taken by biologist Robert White. White's team kept rat brains alive and functioning after detaching them from the body and connecting them to life support. The team claimed:

> [There] is no question that such a preparation should and would demonstrate a level of consciousness and cerebral performance that we have come to expect . . . nor is there any reason we should not expect that the intrinsic individuality, personality, emotional structure, intelligence and memory would not continue to function under these experimental circumstances.[83]

In many ways, biotechnology today is infotechnology. And exploratory biotechnology is burgeoning. Breakthroughs in plastic surgery, prosthetics, redirected cellular activity, and the manipulation of individual atoms is driving advances in everything from cosmetic technology to complex nanosystems. A company called Organogenesis in Canton, Massachusetts, which specializes in the intersection of infotechnology and biotechnology, is involved in "foreskin farming," using cells from infant foreskins to grow human tissue, which is then introduced into a solution of bovine collagen. Artificial muscle has been developed by chemists in Spain using conductive plastic. Lab director Toribio Otero says: "If interfaces are developed between electrical and nervous systems, I think implants of plastic muscles in living creatures will one day be possible."[84] As artificial alternatives become available for a growing range of tissue, it seems only natural that artifical gray matter is not too far in our future.

In that future, alterations of human tissue may result from hormonal and genetic tuning of body growth and function, utilizing genetic learning applied within a single generation. In the long term, nanotechnology, commercial technology for the manipulation of individual atoms, suggests that there will be incredibly fine-tuned ways to move the constituent components of brain and mind. Moravec notes:

> The architecture of the global intelligent network will undoubtedly be quite complex. Various parts of each robot's intelligence will be shared with multiple archiving and knowledge-providing host computers . . . this system will not be a gigantic "superorganism," despite the implied high degree of structural integration. The global "mind" will be compartmentalized . . . the very concept of a center is not applicable to a massively parallel, globally distributed and extremely complex system. [But] this process is accompanied by a widening personal perception of self.[85]

Omega Points

"Collective memory, collective heart; this atmosphere breeds understanding and mutes the ego."

—JIM STARLIN

AS NOTED IN THE PREVIOUS **CHAPTER,** evolutionary transitions are characterized by discontinuity, making it difficult to predict how the evolutionary leap postulated here will manifest in society at large. Russell says: "The Gaia field will not be a property of individual humans any more than [full human] consciousness is a property of individual cells."[1] And although evolutionary transitions are often painted as inevitably positive—there are many modern Utopias in current thinking—modern philosophers are just as comfortable dealing in dystopia, from Huxley's *Brave New World*, to *1984*, to the darker prophets of cyberpunk.

Fundamentalists and conservatives look around their perceived world and see not progress, but social decay. They seek a return to what they perceive as traditional values and assume that society will reform along lines they see as stable and positive. This backward view often seems narrowly focused on the charmed lives of Western, Caucasian males in the 1950s, but chronic problems like economic dislocation, hate crimes, and random violence discourage any belief in real progress.

Nevertheless, I will go right ahead and be a Utopian and, in this chapter, point to some of the outlines of an emerging global consciousness. I will offer some fairly rosy, if not entirely uncritical, predictions of how and why the neurosphere can move humanity toward solutions of some seemingly intractable problems. Just keep in mind what futurist Paul Saffo says: "Never mistake a clear view for a short distance."[2]

GLOBAL INSTITUTIONS

Alexander the Great's construction of a Hellenistic empire was arguably the first institutional manifestation of an evolutionary surge toward unity. Like all empires, it made the fatal mistake of imposing control from without, but it did prove that a culture and mindset could be overlaid across a variety of smaller and disparate geographic states with some degree of continuity. Although we'll discuss the difference between empires and the kind of unity I'm trying to describe here, the persistence of remnants of Alexander's great empire even after his soldiers withdrew indicates some recognition on the part of each local tribe that there is value in being a part of a larger whole. Clearly, humans respond to global institutions that attempt to find a common ground across geographic, ethnic, and religious borders. And they do this even as they vigorously assert and protect their own individual geographic, ethnic, and religious identities.

World Government and the Global Economy

The League of Nations, proposed by U.S. President Woodrow Wilson, was rejected by the United States Congress, which saw in the model of world government something reminiscent of the colonial status it had rejected relatively recently. Wilson was adamant that only a model of unity could address the problems of the world: "There is only one power to put behind the liberation of mankind," he claimed, "and that is the power of mankind. It is the power of the united moral forces of the world, and in the Covenant of the League of Nations the moral forces of the world are mobilized."[3] Despite Wilson's optimism, however, the American public was not ready to pursue his moral vision. After the chastening experience of World War II, however, the United Nations was born. The UN is a far cry from world government, inasmuch as no member gives up sovereignty. Nevertheless, the world body made Americans nervous again in the Reagan years when some Third World countries actually took words like "equality" and "autonomy" seriously.

American fears of a UN "socialist" agenda is, however, just a thinly veiled reaction to the threat of losing access to cheap labor and abundant natural resources in the Third World. U.S. wealth was built on a policy of exploiting our own abundant natural resources without attention to sustainability. That wealth is now sustained by access to cheap foreign natural resources—resources that are kept cheap and accessible by U.S. foreign policy intervention. Noam Chomsky has written whole volumes about how this happens, and exposed the words we use to justify the actions. The end of the Cold War brought the ascendancy of NATO as the only multinational group that could act with any kind of consensus. But NATO looks more like an empire than an organic manifestation of global mind, even granting the assumption that the U.S. is relatively altruistic.

So the United Nations is not world government, anymore than NATO is. But the expansionist and sometimes predatory activity of multinational corporations does constitute a kind of backdoor world government—one that goes by the name of "global economy."

The rise of multinational corporations and their continued consolidation indicate that the world economy increasingly transcends any need for an actual world political structure. This is apparent, for instance, in situations where Western nations attempt to put together a political consensus for military intervention. "The world order, the world market, too-late capitalism, whatever you want to call it, is now alone and triumphant," says anarchist critic Hakim Bey.[4]

In some ways, the fall of the Soviet Union in 1989 marked the true end of the millennium. The frenzy for entrepreneurship that erupted in the wake of the liberation of Eastern Europe and the nations of the former Soviet Union was as exhilarating as any fervor for democracy. Writers like Bruce Sterling note that, ten years later, the defining characteristic of the post-Communist world is naked capitalism—complete with the robber barons and Mafia protection rackets that characterized the United States at the turn of the last century. This may, in fact, be a necessary stage in economic evolution. But that does not disprove the common hunger of humanity for a common set of economic behaviors. McDonald's arches are a powerful symbol of human desire. American companies just happen to be the first to recognize marketing methods that exploit cross-cultural desires and needs.

The acceleration of the movement of capital (mergers, program trading) is enabled by the tendency toward economic unity. Although much capital movement occurs as pure arbitrage and ignores economic development, there is clearly a faster, more fluid marshalling of funds going on that supports positive, real wealth-producing activities.

Billionaire financier George Soros has drawn an explicit link between economic free trade and the political and financial institutions necessary to foster this type of activity. National institutions are necessary before international investors will (or should) welcome fledgling capitalists into the world financial community. Soros formed the Open Societies Foundation to foster these types of institutions. These are, in a sense, institutions of backdoor world government, implemented under a set of financial, rather than political, imperatives. As I write this, China and the U.S. are sparring over China's intense desire to join the World Trade Organization and attain equal trade footing with other members of the world economic community. The argument does not revolve around China's human rights violations, but around China's attempts to retain certain trade barriers.

Modern computer tools clearly support this movement of financial information, enabling investors, in a sense, to "think faster" about these matters and act accordingly. This technology is occasionally vilified, as in the case of the so-called "program trading" that was blamed for the stock market crash of 1987. That crash proved to have very few long-term effects, however, and program trading is alive and well today. In fact, it has merely been incorporated into most investors, planning scenarios.

As noted above, just when you think economic movement can't get any faster, the computer revolution comes along and stomps on the gas pedal. But this raises a number of key questions for our inquiry here. Is the computer revolution just industrial lubrication, or does it signal a more fundamental structural economic change? Is the Internet relegating industry to the status of agriculture—still fundamental, but done more efficiently all the time, until it requires only a small portion of the population to sustain itself? A new business magazine called *Fast Company* documents the "creative destruction" of all manner of industrial-era businesses, from manufacturing to fast food (hyper food?), by the incorporation of information technology and Internet-enabled capabilities.

Job loss caused by automation in this decade may soon dwarf all prior reductions in the work force. In the short run, this can only mean underemployment or unemployment, and other economic dislocations. "Downsizing" is the euphemism used to describe this phenomenon, but the concept inaccurately treats any given corporation as a closed system. In the long run, however, more individuals will be part of the information economy created by this shift, and this can only accelerate the access they have to the infrastructure of the neurosphere.

Economic Concentration

Social critics like Hakim Bey will likely contest the notion that *homo economicus* is universal. The uprising of Chiapas Mayans in protest of NAFTA is sometimes cited as a case in point. I argue that this is a difference in degree rather than kind. Chiapas support groups in this country tend to focus on such mechanisms as coffee-bean collectives that allow indigenous people to preserve their way of life. This belies the theoretical critique, however, which claims that the Chiapas Indians are not economic creatures like any other. In fact, these cooperatives take advantage of the very global financial structure they criticize. Still, these types of cooperative activities do provide useful and important alternatives to a global economic monoculture.

Nevertheless, economic concentration does tend to increase if left unchecked. "Technology opens doors, and oligopoly marches in just behind, slamming them," wrote sociologist Todd Gitlin.[5] Innovation will continue to occur, and the already-wealthy will continue to acquire a disproportionate share of ownership and control of the wealth stemming from that innovation. The disparity between rich and poor is persistent: "The poor are always with us" goes the biblical incantation. Indeed, political debate in the Reagan era often turned on whether the rising tide was lifting all boats, yet the percentage of those under the "official" poverty line in the 1980s was not much different from the period of the Great Depression—or, indeed, throughout most of human history. It may be that, in contemporary American industrial society, there is a feedback mechanism that keeps the disparity in wealth from getting too big: unions form, antibusiness legislation is passed, or the poor and disenfranchised portions of the population simply riot. A character in Tom Wolfe's *The Bonfire of the Vanities* coldly talks about payments being made to minority groups serving as a "pressure valve."

One antidote to this apparent stagnation is what Hazel Henderson called "economic democracy." Economic democrats advocate changes like placing community representatives on boards of corporations, with some kind of political accountability for economic decisions. For instance, if a corporation decides to close a factory, they must subsidize retraining funds. Some may see this as the beginnings of a welfare state. But in some ways, the welfare state is a necessary outgrowth of the dislocations that occur with the swift movement of capital. Welfare programs have been criticized in recent years for being less a safety net and more of an economic "methadone" program. The end of welfare as we know it, however, has not seemed to eliminate the truly needy class. In fact, there seems to be an irreducible minimum of poverty in all modern societies, while the unemployed poor have simply become the working poor.

A less tangible effect of globalization and consolidation is the devastation of the economic base of much of rural America. The trend has spawned a genre of music called No Depression, named after a Woody Guthrie song. A more ominous manifestation of this social feedback is the growth of the so-called Militia Movement, which was responsible for the horror of the

Oklahoma City bombing. These groups, however, are not the answer to the larger question. As William Irwin Thompson points out:

> If all separatist groups were granted national status overnight, the problem of being granted historical representation would not solve the present need for participation in the biospheric politics of the planet. Giving a flag to a nation-state, like giving a club jacket to a gang member, can help, but cannot deal with the post-national politics of the ozone hole or the greenhouse effect.[6]

Information have-nots—those left behind by the technology revolution—embody a persistent critique of the information age. The information economy may ultimately absorb these groups as well, and we should not mistake lack of equal access for no access at all. Despite my optimism, however, there may ultimately be individuals who do not participate in the neurosphere through no choice of their own. We'll explore this tension between the information haves and have-nots below.

The American Empire

U.S. economic primacy in the world has been a "given" for a long time. It was recently estimated that 80 percent of world financial transactions are dollar-based: "The world's foremost transaction currency, its most respected store of value and the reserve currency most widely held by central banks: the mighty U.S. dollar."[7]

Increasingly, economic entropy drives Third World workers to emigrate to the U.S. and, at the same time, drives jobs to cheap labor markets. America, and to some extent smaller Western democracies with "favorite son" multinationals (Thomson in France, Philips in the Netherlands, Nokia in Finland) have induced the rest of the world to play in the same game. The International Monetary Fund, the economic carrot that accompanies the industrial stick, is supported largely by American funds. If the world economy is not American in name, it is American in fact. National sovereignty is preserved in some spheres, but American economic standards are increasingly adopted worldwide. This financial Americanization is paralleled, and in some ways driven, by the export of North American culture.

GLOBAL CULTURE

It is almost axiomatic that most of the world follows American cultural trends. Jack Valenti has observed:

> The U.S. copyright-based industries, including the motion picture, sound recording, computer software, and book industries, were America's number one export sector in 1996. These industries achieved foreign sales and exports of $60.18 billion, surpassing every other export sector, including automotive, agriculture and aircraft.[8]

Sixty percent of all films made worldwide are in English.[9] U.S. television and movie stars are sought by people all over the world. Even when Americans feared Japan's ascent as a new economic power, there didn't seem to be any corresponding fascination with Japanese culture (although the Japanese have proved adept at adopting and economically controlling cultural forms like video games, just as they assumed leadership in the consumer electronics industry). Nonetheless, American celebrities were—and remain—in great demand in Japan for commercials.[10]

The American cultural invasion has not been universally successful, but Hakim Bey notes that those who have resisted the cultural onslaught—Iran, for instance—are conservative or reactionary regimes that impose restrictions on all cultural imports as a matter of social control. "Now there is only revolution in defense of being allowed to be different," Bey claims, citing the Zapatistas in Mexico as an example.[11] Bey would approve of the 1998 bombing of the new Planet Hollywood restaurant in Capetown, South Africa, as an act of pure cultural resistance.

Canada and France are among the few "advanced" nations that insist on a certain percentage of locally produced programming on their national television networks. They fear "cultural colonialism." It is certainly a leap to equate television programming with forms of government or economic activity imposed at gunpoint. But this strong emotional reaction underscores the potency of the exported cultural images in the increasingly shared neurosphere.

In many ways, TV stars are cultural archetypes in the Jungian sense. The characters played by Arnold Schwarzenegger and Clint Eastwood translate easily to foreign cultures. The special effects, action-adventure movies invented by George Lucas are now a template for movies that use shorthand for plot and character and just concentrate on keeping the action going. These archetypal characters and situations, however, are part of an emerging cultural unity accompanying a significant shift in global consciousness. All we can do is hope that the violence, misogyny, and other negative characteristics of these movies do not survive the transition.

Moreover, if the current age of information services is the Third Wave, to use Toffler's phrase, the emerging Fourth Wave may very well involve a revolution in content, or more formally, art. Much of the feeding frenzy of late 1990s Internet capitalism was characterized by information and telecommunication hardware companies desperately trying to acquire "content" and programming, thereby hoping to avoid becoming simply "bit pipes," or conduits for information and content owned, and controlled by others.

And yet no cultural exchange is entirely unidirectional. Clearly, American artists have been busily appropriating various aspects of Third World culture and incorporating it into the matrix of American pop culture. Paul Simon's *Graceland* comes to mind as the most economically successful example of this exchange, as does an entire "world music" category in record stores that didn't exist twenty years ago.

Some culture critics, on the other hand, decry these trends—proof that one man's unity is another's homogeneity. Yet, for better or worse, the ongoing American hegemony of national brands—from 7-11 to Wal-Mart, from McDonald's to Hard Rock Cafe, from Muzak to "alternative" radio formats— is driven by a continual trend toward consolidation. Again quoting Bey, in America we observe "capitulation of the mono-culture on the deepest psychic level."[12] In recent years, I worked in Louisville, Colorado, a community that opened up a large expanse of open land on one side of town for development. In a three-year period—which seemed to go by in an instant—a series of national franchises set up shop, almost completely shutting out locally owned, independent businesses. The almost viral spread of these national chains may have a downside, but consumers clearly respond to what they offer and are being satisfied, for better or worse, by these avatars of common consciousness.

It's hard to be an artistic rebel for very long these days before you are properly formatted and packaged. Very few pop and rock musicians (and I think we can all name most of the exceptions worldwide) even pay lip service to notions of rebellion any more. They start out looking for a record deal. Prepackaged musical acts are launched every year with a whole marketing strategy behind them that treats the music as an afterthought. The Monkees were perhaps the first such group, followed by the Partridge Family, Josey and the Pussycats, Menudo, Spice Girls, Back Street Boys, and a slew of UK "boy bands." And the list, like the beat, goes on. Moreover, this concept of culture as industry has traveled to other cultures. In Japan, prepackaged teenaged singers have become an extremely successful example of this kind of marketing. Finally, a company called Holipro took the ultimate step and created a "virtual" teen idol called Kyoko Date. The singer exists only as a computer generated image, but with all the trappings that make the other "real" stars so popular. (The creation of Lara Croft in computer games is an interesting analogy.)

I cite these examples not to suggest that this kind of thing has a positive value to society, but merely because they represent the growing ease with which such phenomena can be created and propagated within the matrix of converging global consciousness. Even in characterizing this "dark side" as the information society, cultural critic Bey evokes wholeness: "All corporeality reduced to a darkness given shape only by light from the gnostic pleroma, that realm of transcendence from which bodies are exiled: the heaven of glass."[13]

On a more positive note, McLuhan paraphrased Pound thus: "Art is information on how to rearrange your psyche to anticipate the next shock from our extended faculties." That may be true, but the observation is of limited value if art is only available to a few. The culture transmitted by mass media is what will truly impact evolutionary trends, and we may rightly worry about what that means.

GLOBAL MIND AS SOLUTION

The global mind may be able to conceive of and act on solutions to seemingly intractable problems that are the fallout of an increasingly interconnected world. For example, it may be that, following Lovelock, the environmental movement arose as a global feedback mechanism when a sufficient number of people were personally inconvenienced by smelly air and poisoned drinking water. This critical mass of citizenry were then galvanized by a few individuals who crystallized the problem, like author Rachel Carson of *Silent Spring* or David Brower of the Sierra Club. However, as a political proposition, the movement is forever under pressure from industries that are trying to do business more cheaply. Like so very many others, I am convinced that these industries see pollution control strictly as a cost, and will always seek to reduce or eliminate the costs of doing business. So, the question is: Will a global mind be able to see more clearly that environmental protection trumps economic gains, and see through the persistent sophistries that pervade its own common mind?

Projects like Destination Earth, described earlier, seek to provide global entities with a complete environmental profile of the planet. A personalized component can make environmental consequences apparent to individuals who, until now, have acknowledged the plight of the environment only when faced with a local catastrophe. Or, it may make individuals aware of the connection between their own actions and subsequent pollution. If the global mind had an environmental protection component with access to sufficient information, it could function almost like an autonomic nervous system, automatically incorporating the will of individuals to react appropriately to maintain a healthy environment.

Such a desirable outcome is not, however, inevitable. As Ken Wilber points out, in his *Brief History of Everything*: "What computer technology means is the techno-base can support global consciousness, but does not guarantee it."[14] Cyberneticist Francis Heylighen notes the following:

> The values of the Global Brain are simply some kind of an average value of all individuals that are part of it . . . [but] that approach does not help when people hold necessarily opposing values, like when two competitors each want to get the same thing, but only one can have it.[15]

Nevertheless, communication clearly helps. The so-called velvet revolution in many former Iron Curtain nations resulted, in part, from increased knowledge that living conditions were not up to the standards prevailing elsewhere in the world. There is nothing so powerful as an idea whose time has come, especially if accompanied by information that can be acted upon.

SCHOOLS OR EMPIRES

The nihilistic punk era dawned at a time when America was in the grip of a so-called "malaise," its geopolitical influence threatened from Iran to Nicaragua. This malaise reflected a country committed to helping the less fortunate, then suddenly realizing that its own children risked joining the ranks of the less fortunate and living less well than their parents.

One constant refrain heard in the corridors of Congress in the 1990s—mostly among Democrats whose constituents had not yet shared in the financial fruits of the Internet economy—was that America must not become a society of information "haves and have-nots." It is a tribute to American democracy that someone cared enough to raise the issue, but it seems clear that we are already such a society, and were long before computers were invented. Moreover, this may not be a situation we can remedy. Nor is such a goal necessary in order to function collectively. The risk is, rather, that the global mind become merely a "mostly global" mind.

Evolution tells us that some species evolve, while some throw off new species and themselves remain the same. Arthur Clarke's *Childhood's End* posits an evolutionary leap in a single human generation, but it is clear that the old generation that is left behind is the same old human species it always was. John White, who coined the term *homo noeticus* for the next evolutionary step, says "what is happening today is the dominant species is dying out."[16]

One factor at work in the globalization process is that a sufficient number of individual nodes may be required to form a critical mass in order to create a single meta-organism. Some theories of consciousness posit that awareness is a function of the number of brain cells and their consequent interconnections. If this is true, then consciousness has a lower mathematical limit, which some place at 10 billion cells. It may be no coincidence, from our perspective, that the human population is fast approaching that number.

Clearly, only a tiny fraction of those 10 billion people even have telephone service—and that fraction lives largely in developed Western societies. Nonetheless, Moore's Law and parallel developments in wireless bandwidth may combine to effect a rapid transformation. In fact, there is some evidence that people in underdeveloped countries are seizing newly available technologies out of need, then using them increasingly not to destroy, but rather to enhance their indigenous cultures. For example, while there are still many traditional and revivalist performers in the West who avoid electronic instrumentation, other cultures—especially in Africa—have seized upon the electric guitar and synthesizer as a means to enhance and advance their traditional music.

There may also be some willful obstruction intended to block the development of the infrastructure necessary to support the neurosphere. Fundamentalist groups and concerned (and perhaps frightened and ignorant) parents have driven the creation of software that blocks users from many available information sites—not just sites with sexual content, but also sites with points of view not compatible with their own. Such measures can forestall the creation of the critical mass necessary for transformation, but they may also end up creating islands of people disconnected from the larger global mind.

Education for Connection

It may be that the neurosphere will manifest spontaneously when sufficient physical interconnections are made. I believe, however, that the highest quality, the most fully realized neurosphere—one that includes the full preservation of the individual—will only occur through education.

There are larger political forces at play that I believe will be overwhelmed by *homo electric*. Both genetic and environmental forces interact to make some people better at survival and manipulation of tools and resources than others. There are three characteristics that manifest themselves in the better-adapted group: a capacity for isolation, a propensity to teach others out of either altruism or enlightened self-interest, and an instinct to exercise control over other humans as well as the environment. Unfortunately, by acknowledging this fundamental difference between individuals (essentially a difference between smart and stupid, gifted and challenged, talented and ordinary), we open the door to the creation of caste systems, class-based ideologies, and confrontations between nature and nurture. I contend that the emergence of *homo electric* will be a product of education, and that the advent of this new species will depend on its ability to overcome the political, economic, and philosophic powers of our time.

The means for this education are everywhere. The Well, BCN, and even AOL are models of intelligent interconnection. Part of the education, transmission, and nurturing of consciousness is the formation of meta-families and meta-communities that have the tools to process the wealth of information and the closeness to others that is becoming possible.

In order to achieve this interpenetration, however, a minimum of educational attainment may be required. Literacy, perhaps computer literacy, may be one of those minimal requirements. Unfortunately, there are statistics that indicate that the pace at which education is penetrating underdeveloped regions is leveling off. On the other hand, test scores on the whole in advanced Western cultures appear to have rebounded after a steady slide through the 1970s and 1980s.

Education is only half the battle, however. Children may, for many reasons, evolve more quickly than adults. The state of continuing education in our country in particular gives mixed indications of the ability of adult learners to understand and participate in a global mind. The number of noncredit classes in a variety of endeavors has grown, while innovative programs like elder hostels, where the elderly take advantage of college-level instructors and facilities underutilized during the summer, grew at a rapid pace in the 1990s.

One thing, however, is clear. Education for our youth must take advantage of the entertainment values technology can provide in order to capture students' attention. Indeed, there are now many examples of successful "edutainment" being developed by educational institutions in collaboration with the entertainment industry.

Professional educators tend to view large corporate entities bearing gifts with suspicion. Entrepreneur Chris Whittle launched an educational video service called Channel 1, providing news and free televisions in exchange for the right to sell advertising on the channel.[17] The cable television industry's do-good initiative, Cable in the Classroom, gave away free televisions and free cable service, plus a package of noncommercial educational programming. Their pecuniary interest was limited to building some brand loyalty among young audiences over the long term, with a short-term interest of displaying some public spirit in exchange for limited regulation by Congress. Focusing on the financial interests of large media companies, however, fails to reach the real issue.

The commercial media are fighting for the attention of young people, and our schools are too underfunded and understaffed to fight back in a way that keeps young people in school and learning to keep up with a rapidly changing world. This is evident in the way schools in the U.S. have remained largely divorced from the mass media, fostering the impression that the content of education is somehow divorced from popular culture. Likewise, the popular assumption is that adults only need access to current events and will not pursue new accumulations of information in a rigorous way.

More Immediate Media

Integrating media into some kind of personal interface transforms the nature of information processing for the individual. These capabilities demand an information structure that is more interactive, accessible, and retrievable. Even today's Web sites remain signally uncreative in the ways they display and offer information. Indeed, most just look like print media that has been transferred wholesale to a computer screen.

Serial/mosaic newspaper articles are not the best way to attain an understanding of complicated issues. The public's apathy toward political issues is, in part, the result of the way they are reported. One Senate subcommittee vote on defense spending looks pretty much like another; spending went up, spending went down, more battleships, fewer airplanes. The reader has no context in which to consider if this vote is different than any other and is left vaguely wondering: "Didn't we already figure this out?"

The interactive and hypertextual nature of the Web should be able to remedy this. Instead, most Web sites just point you to a series of previous articles, most of which do not contain the text you're after. And to add insult to injury, some newspaper sites charge extra for the privilege of accessing those old, uninformative articles. Even worse, some stories report on issues or situations and then never revisit them, or bury clarifications and follow-up in a small article on page B8.

Even if you wade through a hundred or more articles on a topic or event, can you really synthesize the information in them and identify the actual issues and their status? A really effective Web site would provide an executive summary of all available material and references to previous articles, which are themselves summarized. Better yet, why don't Web interfaces just reinvent the whole concept of a newspaper?

On the television side, social critics like Paul Ehrlich argue that "Mass media could be used to make concepts of consciousness evolution and global consciousness a part of the mental structure of humankind." They stress integration of such messages into the content of programs. Such messages have not been successful in the medium as we know it today—perhaps because they always seem to come in the form of slow-moving, talking-head documentaries.

Some critics have argued that television simply does not lend itself to reform. Others argue that growing up with the ability to change channels on TV helps us develop changing points of view and the ability to hold multiple points of view at the same time. These are adaptive characteristics well suited to the postmodern, fragmented world of today. MTV's Robert Pittman, as noted earlier, posits similar advantages that the current younger generation can gain from television, among them a talent for integrated, nonlinear, multimode processing of information.

These are adaptations of people to the electronic environment. Is it impossible to think that the electronic environment could, in a similar way, adapt to the needs of people? Mass media, for instance, could be made more "Internet-like." Electronic program guides are being developed by print publishers like TV Guide and Internet-based ClickTV that promise to render obsolete the aimless surfing that gave birth to the "least objectionable programming" strategy of the three big broadcast networks. Soon you will be able to search listings—current and future—for appearances of your favorite stars, by subject matter, or by any other feature. You can save programs for later playback. Agent software can gather information on your preferences and evolve over time to find programming of interest to you, even though you haven't specifically requested it. There are now consumer devices, called TiVo or RePlay, that provide digital storage while collecting material through agent technology.

Clearly, technology is becoming available to help people orient themselves in the flood of media and information, and to give them tools for learning and incorporating what they deem necessary. I have no doubt that human ingenuity and the usual collection of human motivations will be sufficient to allow the vast majority of people to keep up with and play in this new collective environment. Intentional participation in this new global mind will grow; but this growth appears to be preceded by activities that occur at the subconscious level.

MIND AT LARGE

"We live in the most active mythogenetic period since the time of the ancient Greeks," says philosopher Michael Grosso. The *X Files* became an immensely popular television show merely by cataloguing the modern mythic bestiary, giving credence to everything from UFOs and extraterrestrials to chupacabras and psychic powers, from near-death experience to crop circles, from visions of the Virgin Mary and shamanism to lycanthropy, ghosts, and government conspiracies. Jacques Valleé, longtime UFO researcher, computer scientist, and determined agnostic, refers to the persistent UFO phenomenon as "folklore in the making." Valleé does not believe in extraterrestrial visitors. His book *Dimensions* lays out logical reasons why the data do not support that hypothesis. The "only truth of UFOs is their effect on us," he argues. He claims that UFO sightings and people's reactions to them "[push] us toward wholeness and a higher conception of mankind."[18] Terence McKenna agrees, claiming, "the extraterrestrial is the human oversoul, in its general and particular expression on the planet."[19]

This view of the wide variety of anomalous phenomena grouped under psychic or occult headings is shared by a number of thinkers. They understand that, despite scientific skepticism, the mass of people respond to these phenomena on a deeper level—the level of myth, the collective unconscious, the level of meaning. Like Valleé, these thinkers view the phenomena as a manifestation of a new conception of humanity.

That odd cases do not fit current scientific models is to be expected. Anomalous data is always what leads the way to newer, better scientific explanations—just as radioactivity led to quantum physics, which in turned proved Newtonian physics to be very incomplete and limited. Thinkers like

Grosso and Valleé see consciousness as a key element of a new conception of physics—a physics, as Valleé put it, that is all about "wholeness." Their assertions place the discussion of these phenomena squarely in the context of this book. I contend that anomalous phenomena are the first definite signs that the neurosphere is taking shape. Their very strangeness is a predictable feature of this new phase of evolution. We can't make sense out of them simply because we are in the middle of the process. Indeed, a small number of researchers have cut through the science-fiction fantasies and the outright pathologies of some "believers" to uncover a core of proven physical phenomena and experiences. These researchers make clear that these phenomena are manifestations of mind that indicate that it can—and does—act in ways that transcend (not "violate") the laws of physics that have been elucidated to date.[20]

In addition, argues Grosso, when taken as a whole, patterns emerge across different phenomena that "appear to constitute a 'message', a message delivered by individuals from what looks like a common, collective source—a 'Mind at Large.'"[21]

Virgins and Aliens

Two books helped crystallize for me the importance of this topic. In his book *Confrontations*, Jacques Valleé summarized several years of research. Despite a similarity of physical effects on alleged UFO witnesses—including burns, bruises, and memory loss—there was wide variation in the witnesses' descriptions of the UFOs—in their shape and their movement through space. Valleé could only identify one consistent piece of evidence—each experience began with a bright light or series of lights. Then I read *Searching for Mary*, in which the author presents portraits of several visionaries who claim regular communication with the Virgin Mary. Each visionary's experiences with Mary began in the same way—with a bright light or series of lights.

I believe, as do Valleé and others, that, in both instances, something real is experienced or perceived. The important difference is in the interpretation the witnesses give to the events. All the Marian visionaries were current or former Catholics, so it is not surprising that their interpretation is Marian. Valleé didn't report religious affiilations, but has noted that UFO witnesses tend to be better educated and well read. Moreover, he theorizes that the speculations of science fiction and theories of extraterrestrial intelligence proposed by sober scientists have created a set of beliefs that may be triggered by the real experiences these witnesses have had.

Beneath these surface dissimilarities, however, lie important patterns in the messages reportedly delivered by both the Virgin Mary and the ETs. These two types of phenomenon may both reveal messages delivered from the unconscious mind of the recipients—and perhaps from the collective unconscious of us all. Indeed, the messages, whether from alien or Virgin, seem to have similar "millenial" content, often suggesting a reward of universal harmony or unity. Similar messages are reported by individuals with LDE—lifeafter-death experiences.

Kenneth Ring, Dennis Stillings, and Michael Grosso are a loosely affiliated group of thinkers who have come to recognize that they are exploring the same phenomena from different angles in different disciplines. I believe their theories tend to support my conclusions that a neurosphere, or a Mind at Large, is forming.

The UFO Contact Experience

Dennis Stillings believes that people are now encountering UFOs "because we have learned everything consequential there is to learn about this material, space-time world and we are bidden by them to take seriously ultra-dimensional, or . . . 'orthogonal' aspects of reality."[22] Likewise, Jacques Valleé proposes that UFOs are a "servomechanism for the growth of human intelligence" and a "control system for human evolution." Their effects are not physical, but felt in our belief systems. "They influence our spiritual life, our culture."[23] Whatever the physical mechanism, "UFOs act as a reality exchange—they trigger a series of symbolic displays out of our collective unconscious."[24] One of Valleé's conclusions was that, even if we discount, as he does, the extraterrestrial hypothesis, clear physical effects have been found and documented in many witnesses.[25] Some researchers have found a tentative link between these events and electrical phenomena, as noted in chapter 4.

Michael Persinger and Paul Devereux have correlated earth lights/UFOs with fault zones in the United States.[26] Persinger theorizes that tectonic pressures preceding earthquakes can generate an electrical field that generates light. Such an electrical field can also directly affect the brains of witnesses to such lights.[27] Persinger believes that UFO encounters are brought about by electromagnetic phenomena and are likely to induce an unusual transient state of activity in the temporal lobe of the brain, like a microseizure, known as temporal-lobe epilepsy.[28]

Devereux's correlation of UFO and other experiences with earth lights caused by seismic activity found two interesting religious correlations, showing that sightings of the Virgin Mary are not the only religious analogs of UFOs. The thousand-year-old home of the great Orthodox monasteries, Mount Athos, is one of Europe's most intense regions of seismic activity.[29] Stonehenge and many other stone circles in England, assumed to be early religious sites, also lie along known fault lines.[30] And if religion was invented by humans to deal with the mystery of death, then another anomalous phenomenon falls right into place here—near-death experiences.

Near-Death Experiences

Near-death experiences, or NDE, have gained a place in the popular consciousness in the last thirty years. Writer Raymond Moody compiled the stories of numerous people who had been pronounced clinically dead, but were then revived, either by medical help or spontaneous activity.[31] The stories of their subjective experiences agree on a number of points:

A sensation of moving rapidly down a long tunnel.

A sensation of having left their physical bodies.

A clear vision of the immediate physical environment, including their own bodies.

A perception that their new "bodies" can move through space.

Visions of spirits of others who have died.

A sense of the presence of a warm spirit, a being of light.

A being who urges them to evaluate their lives; visions of life playing back.

A sensation of approaching the border to the next life.

A perception that the time is not right and they must return, even though they don't want to.

These so-called near-death experiences have spawned a whole field of study. One researcher, Kenneth Ring, observed a similarity between NDEs and UFO close encounters, just as Jacques Valleé had done between UFOs and Virgin Mary sightings.[32] Ring's ambitious conclusion was that the entire Earth is undergoing a planetary near-death experience. Certainly nuclear war, global warming, and other environmental degradations hold the potential of real catastrophe of this nature. (Ring was writing in the 1980s, when the Soviet Union and the U.S. were still building up nuclear arsenals.) Ring viewed UFO messages as a sort of response from the collective unconscious to the threat. NDEs and UFOs, he claimed, are "serving the purpose of jump-stepping the human race to a higher level of spiritual awareness and psychophysical functioning."[33] It is important for us here that Ring explicitly cites Teilhard.

Ring further theorized that features of both experiences, such as dissociation of consciousness from the body, function as psychological defenses. These features may also, in a sense, train individuals to enter these states of consciousness more readily, or at least more comfortably, when they occur.[34] As we will see, when "jacked-in" individuals have a subjective experience of the neurosphere, they may be helped by this kind of training.

People who undergo the trauma of such experiences tend to become "psychological sensitives." They "develop an extended range of human perception beyond normally recognized limits."[35] They tend to have greater sensitivity to and experience a greater likelihood of paranormal events and psychoenergetic effects (such as affecting street lamps). Thus, Ring finds it easy to agree with Devereux that consciousness is a field effect. "Extraordinary encounters appear to be the gateway to a radical, biologically based transformation of the human personality."[36]

Mind at Large

Michael Grosso has spent some time explicating the concept of Mind at Large.[37]

> Mind at Large is the transpersonal aspect of mind; it is distinct from but able to interact with matter. Although our individual minds are constantly interacting with our own bodies, Mind at Large does not normally interact with matter. . . . Mind at Large intervenes at critical junctures: for instance, the origin of life, the development of new and higher species, instances of "paranormal" healing and in other circumstances where we observe psi at work.[38]

Grosso admits it is "futile to invoke psi to explain anything: [I]t is a border concept that marks the limits of current scientific understanding."[39] This is, of course, currently true of any attempt to prove the existence of the neurosphere. But I think these fringes are fertile grounds for seeking its first manifestations.

We should be wary of dismissing the weak grasp on science of many self-styled parapsychologists. Physicists like Robert Jahn have concluded that there is something to these phenomena, and that the shortcoming is not the methodology, but the lack of a good theory:

> The brain is more likely to be a wonderfully complex processing organ. . . . In my opinion, we need to start thinking of consciousness as a field effect, an all-pervading element in the universe, perhaps associated with space-time in ways not currently apparent to us, and affected by the presence of electromagnetism and mass. Such a field would allow the operation of ESP phenomena to be construed in fresh ways.[40]

Grosso proposes that we think of psi ability as a preadaptive structure or organ.

> [B]etter to say psychic functioning is pre-adaptive, leaving the question of organic structure open. . . . And the environment to which psychic functioning is adaptive is a new ecological environment, an environment that Teilhard de Chardin christened the Noosphere.[41]

He invokes the "filter theory" of Henri Bergson—that the brain is normally a filter of Mind at Large, an instrument for adapting to the plane of life on which we live. Sometimes, however, it relaxes its reducing function and permits a greater influx of consciousness from Mind at Large. Bergson speculated that the death of the brain may involve the final breakdown of the filter that opens us to a radically expanded mental space.[42]

Grosso also sees Marian, ET, or NDE visions as manifestations of Mind at Large. In fact, he claims that Ring's theory describes a cause-and-effect relationship between events in human history: "[All] stem from the same adaptive mechanism of the collective unconscious. . . . At Garabandal, [the Virgin] Mary appeared as the intercessor through whom world consciousness may be transformed."[43] Nor are such visions terribly new. Apparitions like those experienced by St. Paul and the Emperor Constantine were answers to a collective crisis: "[T]he cycle of pagan culture was at an end . . . a near death experience of ancient civilization."[44]

Grosso adds:

> Religious beliefs may be durable because the more strongly they are held, the more powerfully they work: that is the more they alter objective reality by means of latent psi. . . . Perhaps there is a relation between religion and parapsychology analogous to the one between astrology and astronomy, or alchemy and chemistry: the former saw in a glass darkly what emerged in the light of empirical discovery.[45]

The paranormal, or psi factor, and the spiritual factor taken together represent the fuller expression of transcendent mind. This is why mystics of great stature frequently show psi powers. If we see these goal-directed epiphanies as showings of Mind at Large—of the collective will of the human species—we can infer a benevolent trait in the evolutionary intelligence. We do not, however, see any signs of omnipotence in the operations of Mind at Large.[46]

Indeed, the evidence seems to be that Mind at Large is actually quite democratic—UFOs, NDEs, and Marian visions are experienced worldwide, by people in all walks of life. Revisiting these themes in his book *The Millenium Myth*, Grosso writes:

> Gaia is attempting to talk with us. Her mind, lacking a taste for Cartesian clarity, communicates in a language of symbols and archetypes. Perhaps the language of crop circles, flying saucers, angels and Marian visions, aliens and men in black. Perhaps we are being signaled from the depths of nature and collective humanity that we are at a fork in the road of time and history.[47]

Is mind as a whole thus struggling to create a new dimension, a new geography, a new environment? Are we collectively creating a new space—a space internal to the imagination of the species, in which we can pursue our evolutionary adventure?[48]

LIMITS AND TRANSCENDENCE

Is the neurosphere forming? Can we see it? How can we better glimpse the onset of this evolutionary transition, apart from sitting on the doorstep awaiting a visit from ET or the Virgin Mary? Does this sound downright ludicrous to you? Then you should remember that poetry and symbolism are often a means of communicating that which will not, or cannot yet, be reduced to linear prose.

An influential writer on these themes, Vernor Vinge, makes this point. Extrapolating from the path of scientific progress, he notes that we ultimately reach a limit. He characterizes the emergence of superhuman intelligence through increased computer augmentation as "the coming technological singularity."[49] In fact, he states flatly that, "[within] thirty years, we will have the technological means to create superhuman intelligence. Shortly after, the human era will be ended."[50]

He calls the limit of this trend a singularity to denote that we cannot see beyond it. The disturbing part for Vinge is that the superhuman intelligence may be the product of a computer bootstrapping itself to create superintelligent machines that leave humanity behind. And it is precisely because they are left behind that merely human minds cannot limn the outlines of that vast future. Vinge's superhuman intelligence is not a conception of neurosphere, but its characterization as a singularity is apposite in terms of how difficult it is to speculate about the nature of the neurosphere.

Cyberneticist Mark Pesce characterizes the difficulty as an application of Godel's incompleteness theorem, which posits that statements about a super-system from within that supersystem are unprovable. The more poetic Michael Grosso makes a similar point: "[We] are struggling with the various ends of the 20th century, the end of God, Philosophy, Art."[51] The preeminence of recycled musical styles by Generation Y may be a signal of this inability to see beyond the inflection point to create the art of a dawning species.

Computer scientist Dave Pape ruefully puts forward an even more sobering thought: "[N]oogenesis began with the very first transfer of information between neurons. . . . It's just that such transfer resulted in a pretty crappy immature global consciousness, like the consciousness of a day old baby."[52] Not only are we unable to see the outlines of this process, he points out, the process itself may be only trivially apparent and may move painfully slowly.

Ego Boundaries

Mark Pesce is a pioneer technologist in the field of virtual reality. He has read Teilhard and is convinced that the neurosphere does indeed exist. In a series of papers and exercises, he hypothesizes what effects may be associated with the neurosphere, then attempts to determine if these effects can be observed and facilitated.

Pesce proposes that one prerequisite for individual participation in the neurosphere is a partial dissolution of ego boundaries:

The traversal from the individual's interior to external expression is the essence of communication. In order to experience the neurosphere, one must be willing to allow some dissolution of one's personal ego boundaries in order to emerge into the larger space of the global mind.[53]

Pesce believes he has seen this happening in an immersive artwork called *OSMOSE*, by Char Davies, which requires the viewer/experiencer to don virtual reality goggles and harness. Movement through the virtual reality is keyed to the individual's breathing cycle—inhale to move upward; exhale to move downward. This alignment leads to a very pleasurable experience for all users, unlike many virtual reality experiences that tend to introduce disorientation or nausea. Participants' reluctance to exit the artwork, Pesce claims, shows a willingness to dissolve ego boundaries.

[This is] an artifact capable of creating a bridge between the unspeakable domain of numinous awareness and the highly circumscribed region of ordinary human perception.[54]

A similar effect is achieved by an art project called *T-VISION*, which essentially reproduces an astronaut's ability to see the Earth as a whole. Pesce, like Frank White (in *The Overview Effect* discussed in chapter 2), believes our experience will lead to a situation in which "the more interaction one has with such a model, the more that one becomes coupled to it, until such time as one's conception of the body of the planet and the model converge." First political boundaries dissolve, then ego boundaries: "[A]n old mystical truth reveals itself as self-evident: all life on Earth is one." Pesce concludes that the ego-dissolving character of these two artifacts provides a path of connection to the neurosphere.

In a similar vein, Peter Russell notes that the Gaia field will not be the property of individual humans any more than consciousness is a property of individual cells: "There is a need for repeated experience of oneness for individuals to be willing to sacrifice ego goals for a united supraself," he points out.[55]

Psychologist Jayne Gackenbush theorizes that children using video games experience a sort of training for ego dissolution:

Children who quickly suspend local spatial referents function more accurately in the video game playing field. . . . Does this ability to simultaneously process various channels of dialogue via chat and to recreate quickly and accurately the virtual space in which they must maneuver mean that they will also move with ease in the realms of the imaginal [i.e. the neurosphere]?[56]

Singing the Neurosphere

So how do we achieve the experience of oneness? I suggested in chapter 1 that we can experience oneness in online communities; but this is not the only way. Indeed, unable to convince my own wife that the Well is fun, I have reluctantly concluded that sitting at a computer and typing just does not look like fun to everyone—at least, not from the outside.

There are other communal experiences, however, that are not mediated by technology. Certainly, everyone knows the horror stories of communal cults like the Manson Family, the Branch Dividians, or Heaven's Gate. As destructive as these cults were, they did demonstrate the ability of people to lose their identities in a larger whole. By contrast, there were (and are) psychedelic communes that do not encourage psychosis—groups like The Farm, which testifies to the experience of "intersubjectivity," or the personal experience of some other person's subjective experience. Intersubjectivity was mediated at first by psychedelic drugs, but soon manifested without chemical assistance. In fact, the communal impulse has a long history in this country, ranging from the Oneida Community to the Shakers. Likewise, several Native American tribes had no notion of individual property or of any behavior that was not an expression of tribal beliefs as a whole.

Several attempts are now surfacing, consciously or unconsciously, to engender experiences that help manifest an experience of neurosphere and still have some fun in the process. Mark Pesce and several colleagues created one such effort called The WORLDSONG Project, wherein peace is explicit:

WORLDSONG intends to produce an unusual effect; consciousness of the neurosphere. . . . [It] uses conferencing technologies to produce a realtime, spatialized environment for singing, chanting and toning, either singly or in unison with others. Participants can register their location on the surface of the globe, and can participate or just listen to the "group song." . . . Eventually the interface capabilities will allow a participant to wander through WORLDSONG space by wearing a device which tracks position and orientation, making it possible to traverse the world-space of the participant singers by traversing a physical environment. Then it will then be possible to "walk the globe" in and through this song-space.[57]

WORLDSONG is just one of a number of artifacts that seek to externalize the interior of the neurosphere. Pesce indicates that, confronted with the existence of a cybernetic superbeing, we must begin to develop ways to communicate with it: "[W]e need a noosphone."WORLDSONG has the further advantage of operating at the preconscious, symbolic level where humans respond to music, often acknowledged as the universal language: "[Aural] travel through our planet's realtime symphony can create deep feelings of global continuity and exploration."[58]

A related metaphor and mechanism is offered by Anthony Judge,[59] who theorizes that, just as cars were once referred to as horseless carriages, similar metaphors may limit our comprehension of what's happening now. Although the "information superhighway" metaphor proved limited and has faded from usage, it did capture a geographic feel that seemed to work for people. Bookmark lists and other techniques employing verbal or computer metaphors seem to fall short of giving users maps of the world they are learning. Eric Raymond has noted that the metaphor implicit in the term "home page" ". . . is a territorial claim in the neurosphere."[60] Indeed, it is customarily recognized as such—note that "addresses," called "domain names," can be owned and legally protected. These are "assimilable to our instinctive notions of territory and property but only after some effort . . . our instinctive wiring about territory."[61]

A suitably geographic—yet immersible—metaphor, says Judge, may come from indigenous aboriginal Australians. They can recreate the world in "dreamtime" and wrap it "in a web of song." Aborigines treat the landscape as a form of physical musical score, calling their traditional trails "songlines."

These are a powerful memory aid to navigation over the Earth and the location of essential resources, as well as providing a continuing rehearsal of cultural history. A songline is therefore a succession of sites along a track "vibrant with incident power and meaning" allowing for a dramatic and aesthetic participation in the environment.[62]

Similar geographical metaphors from around the world—ley lines and feng shui, for example—are often said to link sacred sites. So why is it hard to accept that the World Wide Web may link sites of great meaning or sacredness?

Judge seeks to develop methods that trace a sacralized path through the World Wide Web, thereby seeking a personal understanding of globality. In other words, a particular path through the Web may be characterized and experienced as a particular melody. Pesce believed that such methods would allow intuitive and internalized understanding and continual cognition of the reality of the global brain.

The World Wide Web as Super Brain

Mark Pesce has also written that, "the world wide web is the signifier of the neurosphere." Likewise, Marc Andreeson describes the invention of the graphical Web browser Mosaic thus: "[T]he pent-up stresses connected to the formation of the neurosphere violently, instantaneously and ubiquitously released." It's hard to argue with that observation. The bursting forth of the Web and phenomena like Web-mania on Wall Street looks for all the world like Teilhard's supersaturated solution, changing phases in an evolutionary nanosecond.

Thus it may be fitting to close this book with a look at attempts to fit the Web to biological models of organism and consciousness. Perhaps by doing so, we can discern what technical or behavioral developments may hasten a more conscious, helpful, and meaningful neurosphere.

Francis Heylighen and Johan Bollen have made one such attempt.[63] They took as a point of departure some simple correspondences:

Web documents → Neurons

Hypertext links → Synapses

Web documents → Concepts

Hypertext links → Semantic associations between concepts

This represents an interesting first step, although their correspondences were never developed. The following extension doesn't seem to have any neurobiological underpinning:

Web documents	→ Neurons	→ Concepts
Hypertext links	→ Synapses	→ Semantic associations between concepts

There is no evidence, for example, that concepts are stored in individual neurons or have any such one-to-one correspondence. Nonetheless, the first set of correspondences is useful as a point of departure for speculation about how to build a more organic World Wide Web—one that acts as an organism, and perhaps even as a brain.

The first requirement for treating the Web as a brain is already accomplished. All parts of the network communicate via the same protocol. So is a second step that links documents through a network of associations or webs similar to the associative memory of the brain. And distributed computing is the foundational infrastructure that allows transparent global access to all information from anywhere.[64]

The next phase of development may already be in its infant stages. Associative learning occurs as the brain groups similar concepts over time. The Web needs a similar mechanism to strengthen links that are used frequently and weaken ones that are not. Eventually, new documents will be linked automatically to logical areas. In fact, Heylighen and Bollen created an algorithm to do just that. As a result, they observed the self-organization of a semantic network. One strength of this approach is that it works locally; each link need only worry about the links one or two steps away. Mimicking nature, the structure self-organizes globally.

Moving to an even higher level of complexity, we can consider how the Web approximates thinking or problem solving, capabilities that require that we move beyond search engines to something like agent technology. Agents can be a mechanism for spreading activation. For example, one concept activates an adjacent concept—"pets," for instance, leads to "animals." An active mind can search along relevant paths until it finds the desired solution.

Agents then become learning agents—they figure out successful past strategies and activate those more quickly in the future.

> [The] agents searching the Web, exploring different regions, creating new
> associations by the paths they follow and the selections they make, and com-
> bining the found information into a synthesis or overview that either solves
> the problem or provides the starting point for a further round of reflection,
> seem wholly analogous to thoughts spreading and recombining over the net-
> work of associations in the brain. This would bring the Web into the meta-
> system of thinking.[65]

Agent technology continues to develop on the Web. General Magic, Firefly,
and other companies have created agents that can function for the user as a
sort of unconscious activity, finding content you like even though you didn't
ask for it, and working while you do other things with your conscious attention. Push technology then brings the content to you when you are ready, or
interrupts you if the information is urgent.

The next level for Heylighen and Bollen is metarationality—the capacity to
create new concepts, rules, and models, and thus change a way of thinking. It
is the discovery of general principles for situations not yet observed:

> A metarational Web would continuously check the coherency and complete-
> ness of the knowledge it contains. If it finds contradictions or gaps, it would
> try to situate the persons most likely to understand the issue and direct their
> attention to the problem.[66]

The final stage for Heylighen and Bollen is the "integration" of individuals, which I discussed at length in chapter 4. To use the cognitive power of
the Web effectively, we must reduce the distance between it and the user:

> With a good enough interface, there should not be a difference between
> internal and external thought processes. . . . The question remains whether
> individuals would agree to be so intimately linked into a system they only
> partially control. On the one hand, individuals might refuse to answer a
> request from the super brain. On the other hand, no one would want to miss
> the opportunity to use the unlimited knowledge and intelligence of the
> superbrain for solving one's own problems. However, the basis of social
> interaction is reciprocity. People will stop answering your requests if you
> never answer theirs.[67]

Brewster Kahle, an Internet pioneer who invented search engines before there was a World Wide Web, recently created (and sold) a company called Alexa. This outfit commercialized the function Heylighen and Bollen equate to associative learning. The Alexa service informs the user as the user surfs to Web sites. It will tell you about other related sites, what other users have thought about the site, and how long they spend there. The more people who use a site, the stronger the referral to that site for new users. You can also add comments or "signposts" that let other users follow you from one site to another. All of this builds a web of interactions between users that will, ultimately, serve as feedback for the building of underlying content and infrastructure, strengthening associations that people deem important. These are the "songlines" and "feng shui" of the modern telecommunication infrastructure as internalized by humanity.

Philosophical Reflections on the Omega Point

Despite the signposts, speculation about a future neurosphere remains fuzzy. Consider the following excerpts from disparate philosophers:

> Individual soul, like group soul, is immortal, but its task is to transcend rather than repeat previous experience. Soul is currently involuntary and unconscious, it will later evolve to spirit, voluntary and conscious. . . . The evolutionary force in man is the promise of self-transcendence.[68]

> We've created a situation in which the imagination is something we can share. . . . We have the possibility of living in our own past, or of creating and trading realities as art. Art as life lived in the imagination is the great archetype that rears itself up at the end of history. . . . [Ultimately,] the World Soul may actually gauge the finite life of the sun, and it may be trying to build a lifeboat for itself to cross to another star.[69]

> In man, the hitherto chromosomic becomes primarily Noospheric—transmitted not by genes but by the surrounding environment . . . severe demographic pressure also requiring improved Reflection. . . . Humanity is building its composite brain beneath our eyes— may it tomorrow find its heart. [70]

The mystery of life is an organic outgrowth of the core forces of electromagnetic and gravitational fields. Domesticated primates have erected an elaborate superstructure around the dance of matter and energy, and the transmission of genetic code messages over times exceeding individual life spans. And how is it that, in that simple pursuit, we make that successful transmission of code so painful?

The secret doesn't have to reside in a "god" in a remote heaven, or in some abstract, hyperdimensional Jehovah. One way to think of the neurosphere may be simply as a One World Friendship. To what will you look for help, if not to that which is greater than yourself? And the simple truth is that "You-plus-Me" is greater than "Me."

A considerable conversation (the word "considerable" here translates as "bringing stars together") can grow and strengthen the beginnings of *homo-electric*. This may happen on the Well, or at some other crossroad of conversation. You may find, as I did, that that conversation begins in a higher human language. Whether it be through integrated multimedia or crop circles, we need better ways to express where we want to go.

More than anything, however, we must get busy. We must find the modern schools and networks of the like-minded. We must start practicing varieties of unity.

See you in there.

Afterword

9/11—A World at War with Itself

"If all men were brothers, would you let one marry your sister?"

—THEODORE STURGEON

DO THE EVENTS OF 9/11 and beyond represent a brutal refutation of Teilhard's visions of progress and unity? Or are they just the first evidence that what Teilhard foresaw is coming to pass? I believe the answer is the latter, as revealed by a complex weave of war, technology, history, and spirituality.

The war on terror, as proclaimed by President Bush, is an incipient form of conflict within the neurosphere—not across borders, but within the skin of a single global entity. That war will not be confined to Afghanistan, or Iraq, or any small collection of countries. The Al Qaeda network is said to operate within more than sixty countries. It is a stunning fact that they operated most successfully in Florida, a state upon which it will be hard for Mr. Bush to declare war. And it seems increasingly clear, after a year of this war, that the supply of fresh recruits to the terrorist cause continues to grow.

So how do you find and defeat this enemy within? On one front of the war, Richard Clarke, new cyberspace security adviser to the president, says, "We must secure our cyberspace from a range of possible threats." How do we secure an asset whose value comes precisely, like airline travel, from its openness and ubiquity? How do we secure an asset whose value, says Bob Metcalfe in his description of the network effect, increases exponentially with the number of computers—or conscious nodes—connected to it?

At the November 2001 Comdex trade show, the Mecca of computer geeks, companies slammed together last-minute market-positioning software and hardware as solutions for law enforcement and terror prevention. One concept that may be helpful is data mining—the technical approach at the core of Carnivore. This was once considered a paranoid fantasy, but has since been confirmed as a government initiative to monitor all Internet traffic for signs of crime. This technique is not fundamentally different from that employed by search engines like Yahoo, Ask Jeeves, or Google. What makes the technique relevant to our discussion is the assumption that so much human activity is now represented in one form or another on the Internet, and that, therefore, the mass of Web pages, chat rooms, and email logs, is a unified entity within which all information resides. Did I say an entity?

Perhaps the Web is, at most, only a metaphor of human activity. Yet it is searchable. All that is good or evil in the world, or any subset of the world that it represents, can be "mined" from within it. The Web underscores the interconnectedness that is here now, and growing.

The Panopticon, a surveillance technology of the 21st century (although the term was coined in the 19th), is about to be unleashed without the niceties of protected civil liberties or the illusion of privacy. This will mean that someone can be watching you, but also that you can be watching everyone. For every knee-jerk libertarian encrypting his banal emails, there is a Webcam exhibitionist begging you to look and see. We can run, but we can't hide— and perhaps we shouldn't try. The march of technology is inexorable. It is part of human nature. And for those who scoff and point to the majority of the world still without electricity, let alone Internet access, I point to the ability of the poorest desert nomad to access Kalishnikov technology all too easily. And that is where history comes in.

Francis Fukuyama, who, with the fall of the Soviet empire, posited "the end of history," was proclaimed irrelevant by competing pundits. But after 9/11, Fukuyama wrote, "I remain right. Modernity is a very powerful freight train that will not be derailed by recent events, however painful. . . . The progress of mankind over the centuries toward modernity, is characterized by institutions like liberal democracy and capitalism."[1] What is missing from this formulation, of course, is a broader view of the range of human behavior. Democracy and capitalism are, I agree, the most efficient behaviors for achieving the equitable allocation of scarce resources. But its benefits are, unfortunately, strictly limited to domains external to the human.

Islamic fundamentalism is attractive precisely because it offers to fill a need for those who exist in repressive regimes beyond the reach of these benefits. That need lies beyond politics and economics, in a third realm of human existence—spirituality. Unless we harness the long view of progress in the political and economic realms to the aspirations of this third realm, there will be no meaningful progress. Hence the angst of modern American life. Having just gone through another capitalist Christmas, I am happy for the materialist gifts that my children understand and need on a fundamental level. I remember, however, that they are a distant second to parental love and care, and are driven by deeper meaning. I find that I, myself, with so much time taken up by daily work and constant parenting, have only enough left to go and buy a few trinkets for myself. But when I consider this, I recognize how these actions leave me fundamentally unsatisfied.

Democracy at its best allows for the freedom of religion, but it does not guarantee its efficacy. My wife, who was not raised in a religious belief system, grew to place her faith in civic institutions, and saw her ethics reflected and served there. She is an unreconstructed liberal Democrat who believes there are fundamental human values that we, as fellow members of the body politic, can negotiate, defend, and reinforce through a 200-year-old system of representative government. With 9/11, however, this belief system failed her. This was not just progress delayed by a reactionary coalition, but the seeming death of progress itself.

She started going to churches, sampling a range of denominations—mostly Christian, but some not subscribing to any of the monotheistic traditions. But she has found that all of them fall short, whether in dogma or in ritual. Her impulse, however, was fundamental. It is an impulse common to us all. It is the urge—as basic as food or sex—to seek meaning, to seek a pattern in the chaos. Even my five-year-old in kindergarten responds easily and happily to her teacher's directive to raise her hand whenever she sees a pattern in any of their daily activities. Perhaps the journey to the neurosphere, a whole in which literally everything is part of the pattern, can provide that purpose, if only we take a broad enough and long enough perspective.

To suggest to a Muslim or a Christian that the advent of the neurosphere is the next logical step in religious practice for them is a scary proposition—especially for those who have been beaten down at the wrong end of the democratic and capitalist systems. Their religion is the only thing they have in which they can believe—the only thing flexible enough in their minds to act as a support. Jesus always forgives. When others say you are a loser, Jesus knows you are not. With Allah, all things are possible. And the paradise that is guaranteed to all, as long as they believe, is irresistible, because belief is something that is always the bedrock, the last resort, the final possession of which an individual can never be stripped, because it is always inside.

I don't know how the neurosphere will help these people. But I want to try to convince them that each of them, even the most miserable and destitute, is an equally important part of this massively parallel, loosely affiliated, but still cohesive 6-billion-parts-strong *Being*. All of us together, we *are* God. I don't care what word you use to describe it, just don't tell me my concept of it is wrong. And don't tell anyone else that they are not a part of it.

This is one system that can not allow exclusion. There are no infidels, no heretics, in the neurosphere. You are part of it whether you acknowledge it or not. And so is your worst enemy. Moreover, until you liberate him or her(and perhaps therein lies the kernel of a more humane foreign policy), you yourself will never be free. You will never take that next step into paradise. Here on Earth, wherever, whenever. Amen. In'shallah.

So maybe it all comes down to compassion—in foreign policy and in everyday life. Can we get there? Maybe not. Noted pundit Paul Krassner may be right: "The final war will be fought between those who believe all is one and those who don't."

Maybe. But if it comes down to that, I know which side I'll be on.

Notes

Chapter 1

1. R. U. Sirius and Jude Milhon, *How to Mutate and Take Over the World* (New York: Ballantine Books, 1996), p. 286.

2. David Cox, posting at *http://www.cinemedia.net/dma/emu* (accessed March 1999; site now discontinued).

Chapter 2

1. Fitz Hugh Ludlow, *The Hasheesh Eater* (New York: Harpers, 1857), p. 312.

2. Mary Lukas and Ellen Lukas, *Teilhard: A Biography* (New York: McGraw Hill, 1977), p. 50.

3. Letter quoted in Lukas and Lukas, *Teilhard: A Biography*, p. 50.

4. Pierre Teilhard de Chardin, *The Phenomenon of Man* (New York: Harper Colophon, 1975).

5. Teilhard de Chardin, *The Phenomenon of Man*, p. 20.

6. Teilhard de Chardin, *The Phenomenon of Man*, p. 146.

7. Teilhard de Chardin, *The Phenomenon of Man*, p. 127.

8 . Teilhard de Chardin, *The Phenomenon of Man*, p. 222.

9 . Teilhard de Chardin, *The Phenomenon of Man*, p. 87.

10 . Teilhard de Chardin, *The Phenomenon of Man*, p. 264.

11 . Teilhard de Chardin, *The Phenomenon of Man*, p. 172.

12 . Teilhard de Chardin, *The Phenomenon of Man*, p. 221.

13 . Teilhard de Chardin, *The Phenomenon of Man*, p. 182.

14 . J.B.S. Haldane, "Essay on Science and Ethics" in *The Inequality of Man* (London: Chatto & Windus, 1932), quoted in Teilhard de Chardin, *The Phenomenon of Man*, p. 57.

15 . Teilhard de Chardin, *The Phenomenon of Man*, p. 240.

16 . See, for example, discussion in John Brockman, *The Third Culture*, (New York: Simon and Schuster, 1995).

17 . Teilhard de Chardin, *The Phenomenon of Man*, p. 246.

18 . Teilhard de Chardin, *The Phenomenon of Man*, p. 257.

19 . Peter Russell, posting on Global Brain mail list (accessed July 2003; archived at *http://pespmc1.vub.ac.be/*).

20 . Heylighen, posting on Global Brain mail list (accessed September 2003; archived at *http://pespmc1.vub.ac.be/*).

21 . Teilhard de Chardin, *The Phenomenon of Man*, p. 262.

22 . Jim Starlin, *Warlock*, 1:15 (New York: Marvel Comics, 1978), p. 9.

23 . Teilhard de Chardin, *The Phenomenon of Man*, p. 244.

24 . Teilhard de Chardin, *The Phenomenon of Man*, p. 125.

25 . See, for example, D. M. Armstrong, *A Materialist Theory of the Mind* (London: Routledge & Kegan Paul, 1968).

26 . Richard L. Gregory ed., *The Oxford Companion to the Mind* (Oxford: Oxford University Press, 1987), p. 165.

27 . Toward a Science of Consciousness conference Web site can be accessed at *http://consciousness.arizona.edu/*.

28 . David Chalmers, "Facing Up to the Problem of Consciousness," in *Journal of Consciousness Studies*, 2(3):200–19, 1995.

29 . See, for example, Charles Tart, ed., *Transpersonal Psychologies* (New York: HarperCollins, 1983, 1992).

30 . John Lilly, *The Center of the Cyclone* (New York: Julian Press, 1972).

31 . This discussion is based in part on articles in Brockman, *The Third Culture*.

32 . Brockman, *The Third Culture*, p. 215.

33 . Brockman, *The Third Culture*, p. 349.

34 . Lewis Thomas, *The Lives of a Cell* (New York: Viking Press, 1974), p. 13.

35 . Thomas, *The Lives of a Cell*, p. 13.

36 . Thomas, *The Lives of a Cell*, p. 14.

37 . Thomas, *The Lives of a Cell*, p. 112.

38 . John Champagne, summary of Evelyn Strauss, "Mob Action: Peer Pressure in the Bacterial World," *Science News*, August 23, 1997.

39 . Willis Harman, *Global Mind Change* (New York: Warner Books, 1988).

40 . Harman, *Global Mind Change*, p. 30.

41 . William Irwin Thompson, *Imaginary Landscape: Making Worlds of Myth and Science* (New York: St. Martin's Press, 1989).

42 . Thompson, *Imaginary Landscape*, p. 71.

43 . Thompson, *Imaginary Landscape*, p. 143.

44 . Thompson, *Imaginary Landscape*, p. 136.

45 . Thompson, *Imaginary Landscape*, p. 81.

46 . Lankavatara Sutra, translation in Dwight Goddard, ed., *A Buddhist Bible* (Boston: Beacon Press, 1966).

47 . Robert A. F. Thurman, trans., *The Tibetan Book of the Dead: The Book of Liberation through Understanding of the Between* (New York: Bantam, 1994).

48 . Thurman, *The Tibetan Book of the Dead*, p. 28.

49 . Thurman, *The Tibetan Book of the Dead*, p. 37.

50 . Thurman, *The Tibetan Book of the Dead*, p. 55.

51 . Commentary on the Avatamsaka Sutra in Stephen Mitchell, ed., *The Enlightened Mind* (New York: Harper and Row, 1989).

52 . Ken Wilber, *The Atman Project* (Wheaton, IL: Quest Books, 1980).

53 . Wilber, *The Atman Project*, p. 29.

54 . Wilber, *The Atman Project*, p. 49.

55 . Wilber, *The Atman Project*, p. 49.

56 . This discussion is based on Gershom Scholem, *Kabbalah* (New York: Meridian, 1978).

57 . Exhibit at Pirate: A Contemporary Art Oasis, 1982.

58 . Carl Jung, *Archetypes and the Collective Unconscious* (Princeton: Princeton University Press, Bollingen Paperback Edition, 1980), p. 4.

59 . Erich Neumann, *The Origins and History of Consciousness* (Princeton: Princeton University Press, Bollingen Series, 1954).

60 . This summary is from Dolores E. Brien, "Psychology and Technology: Archetypes of the Internet" (accessed April 2005, archived at *www.cgjung.com*).

61 . Ralph Abraham Keynote Lecture (author's notes on lecture at Telluride Mushroom Festival and Conference, 1995).

62 . Ralph Abraham Keynote Lecture (author's notes on lecture at Telluride Mushroom Festival and Conference, 1995).

63 . Frank White, *The Overview Effect* (Boston: Houghton Mifflin, 1987).

64 . White, *The Overview Effect*, p. 216.

65 . Rudy Rucker, in *Seek!* (New York: Four Walls Eight Windows, 1999), says that, in Silicon Valley, "I felt a real sense of being engaged in a Great Work, in something like the same way that the workers on the Notre Dame Cathedral might have felt" (p. 197).

66 . Harman, *Global Mind Change*, p. 87.

67 . White, *The Overview Effect*, pp. 56–57.

68 . Olaf Stapledon, *The Starmaker* (London: Methuen and Company, 1937; reprint Dover Publications, 1968), p. 297.

69 . Stapledon, *The Starmaker*, p. 328.

70 . Stapledon, *The Starmaker*, p. 348.

71 . Stapledon, *The Starmaker*, p. 405.

72 . Stapledon, *The Starmaker*, p. 429.

73 . Stapledon, *The Starmaker*, p. 410.

74 . Christina Grof, *The Thirst for Wholeness* (New York: HarperSanFrancisco, 1993).

75 . Stewart Brand, ed., *The Last Whole Earth Catalog* (New York: Random House, 1971).

76 . Richard Dawkins, *The Selfish Gene* (Oxford: Oxford University Press, 1976; reprint 1978), pp. 206, 208.

77 . Dawkins, *The Selfish Gene*, p. 213.

78 . Robert Ornstein and Paul Ehrlich, *New World New Mind* (New York: Doubleday, 1989).

79 . Ornstein and Ehrlich, *New World New Mind*, pp. 28, 36, 48.

80 . Ornstein and Ehrlich, *New World New Mind*, p. 5.

81 . Ornstein and Ehrlich, *New World New Mind*, p. 80.

Chapter 3

1 . Marshall McLuhan, *The Gutenberg Galaxy* (London: Routledge & Kegan Paul, 1962), p. 31.

2 . Marshall McLuhan, *Understanding Media* (New York: McGraw-Hill, 1964).

3 . Gordon Moore, "Cramming More Components onto Integrated Circuits," *Electronics,* 38, (no. 8), April 19, 1965. Technically, the original observation refers to the doubling of the number of transistors per integrated chip.

4 . *Multichannel News*, August 16, 1999.

5 . Executive Summary 1993.

6 . Tim Berners-Lee, "The World Wide Web: A Very Short Personal History," at *www.w3.org/People/Berners-Lee/ShortHistory*.

7 . For more information, see Grameen Bank Web site at *www.grameen.com*.

8 . Quoted in program of RealTime Conference, produced by *Fast Company* magazine, October 1999.

9 . Marcos Novak, "Liquid Architectures in Cyberspace," *Cyberspace: First Steps*, Michael Benedict, ed. (Cambridge, MA: MIT Press, 1992), p. 225.

10 . See archive at *www.liveworld.com/transcripts/publishers/WingspanBank.html*.

11 . Michael Grosso, *The Millenium Myth* (Wheaton, IL: Quest Books, 1995), pp. 261, 270.

12 . *New York Times*, January 24, 1990.

13 . Web site at *http://www.terraserver.com*. The company acquired images from the commercial arm of the Russian Aviation and Space Agency.

14 . Web site at *http://www.setiathome.ssl.berkeley.edu*.

15 . Cinnamon Twist, *The Imaginal Rave* at *http://www.hyperreal.org/raves/spirit/vision/Imaginal_Rave.html*.

16 . Paul Saffo (archives at *http://www.saffo.org*).

17 . Web site at *http://www.xybernaut.com*. See also online at
http://www.wearcam.org/mann.html
and *media.mit.edu/projects/wearables/lizzy/*

18 . Steve Mann Web site at *http://www.wearcam.org/mann.html*.

Chapter 4

1 . Wilder Penfield, *The Mystery of the Mind: A Critical Study of
Consciousness and the Human Brain* (Princeton, NJ: Princeton
University Press, 1978).

2 . Steve Solomon, comments to author on draft manuscript, July
1989.

3 . Web site at *http://pr.caltech.edu/media/lead/102797JP.html*.

4 . "Connecting Brains to Computers: The Neuroprobe,"
http://www.neuro.gatech.edu/groups/potter/pinelab.html.

5 . This research description is no longer online. Current work by this
research group is now at *http://www.its.caltech.edu/~halweb/*.

6 . Current work by this group, the Center for Neuromorphic
Engineering, may be found at *http://www.erc.caltech.edu/*.

7 . "Microstimulators and Microtransducers for Functional
Neuromuscular Stimulation," principal investigator Joel Schulman,
http://www.ninds.nih.gov/funding/research/npp/sow/mustm.htm.

8 . See also the Human Machine Design Laboratory Web site at *http://www.me.umn.edu/labs/hmd/index.shtml*. Incidentally, even the development of artificial muscles is based on work in the electrical realm. Smart gel made from piezoelectric polymers has been successfully developed at MIT for artificial muscle. An electric charge initiates movement.

9 . Reuters News Service, August 26, 1998.

10 . *Red Herring*, April 1999, referencing AP story October 1998.

11 . *Defense News*, March 1995, reporting on work at the Naval Research Laboratory.

12 . Robert Becker, *Cross Currents* (Los Angeles: Jeremy P. Tarcher; New York: distributed by St. Martin's Press, 1990), p. 46. Also, there is a correspondence between the body's electrical characteristics as measured by L-fields and the meridians of acupuncture—thus the Chinese concept of chi energy. See Michael Shallis, *The Electric Connection* (New York: New Amsterdam, 1988), p. 185.

13 . Shallis, *The Electric Connection*, p. 111.

14 . Shallis, *The Electric Connection*, p. 121.

15 . Becker, *Cross Currents*, p. 140.

16 . Becker, *Cross Currents*, p. 32.

17 . Becker, *Cross Currents*, p. 53.

18 . Web site at *http://www.niehs.nih.gov/emfrapid/booklet/emf2002.pdf*.

19 . Becker, *Cross Currents*, p. 53.

20 . A National Cancer Institute study in 1998 further tips the scale toward "not a major and probably not even a minor component to the cause of cancer." *Washington Post*, 1998.

21 . Rupert Sheldrake, *A New Science of Life* (Los Angeles: Jeremy P. Tarcher; New York: Distributed by St. Martin's Press, 1987).

22 . Arthur Young, *The Reflexive Universe* (New York: Delacorte Press, 1976).

23 . Shallis, *The Electric Connection*, pp.114, 243.

24 . Shallis, *The Electric Connection*, p. 244.

25 . Web site at *http://www.aapb.org/i4a/pages/index.cfm?pageid=3336*.

26 . "Brain/Computer Interface Now MAX Compatible," at *http://news.harmony-central.com/Newp/2002/IBVA-for-MAX.html*.

27 . Web site at *http://www.aquathought.com/briefing/immerse.html*.

28 . See abstracts of various publications on National Institutes of Health Web site, Medline database, at *http://www.nlm.nih.gov*.

29 . Michael Grosso, *The Final Choice* (Walpole, NH: Stillpoint Publishing,1985), p. 85.

30 . Nick Herbert, *Elemental Mind* (New York: Dutton, 1993), p. 182.

31 . Herbert, *Elemental Mind*, p. 239.

32 . John Eccles, *Proceedings of the Royal Society*, 227B 411.

33 . C.J.S. Clarke, "The Nonlocality of Mind," *Journal of Consciousness Studies*, 2 (3): 231, 1995.

34 . Robert Jahn and Brenda Dunne, "Science of the Subjective," *Journal of Scientific Exploration*, 11(2):201–224, 1997.

35 . Michael Murphy, *The Future of the Body* (New York: Jeremy P. Tarcher, 1992).

36 . Murphy, *The Future of the Body*.

37 . Shallis, *The Electric Connection*, p. 244.

38 . Shallis, *The Electric Connection*, p. 24.

39 . Shallis, *The Electric Connection*, p. 41.

40 . Shallis, *The Electric Connection*, p. 58.

41 . Shallis, *The Electric Connection*, p. 21.

42 . Hilary Evans, *The SLI Effect* (London: ASSAP, 1993).

43 . Anonymous posting on the Well, March 1993.

44 . *New York Times*, October 29, 1997.

45 . Shallis, *The Electric Connection*, p. 36.

46 . Paul Devereux, *Earth Lights Revelation* (London: Blandford Press, 1989), p. 208.

47 . Fitz Hugh Ludlow, *Vanity Fair Magazine*, January 1861.

48 . Murphy, *The Future of the Body*, p. 36.

49 . Web site at *http://www.nssl.noaa.gov/edu/ltg*.

50 . Shallis, *The Electric Connection*, pp. 102, 118.

51 . Shallis, *The Electric Connection*, p. 195.

52 . Devereux, *Earth Lights Revelation*, citing Tributsch, p. 51.

53 . Michael Persinger, "The Tectonic Strain Theory," Web site at *http://www.laurentian.ca/neurosci/_people/Persinger.htm*. Also cited in Devereux, *Earth Lights Revelation*, p. 188.

54 . Albert Paul Krueger and Eddie James Reed, "Biological Impact of Small Air Ions," *Science*, September 1976, p. 1209.

55 . Devereux, *Earth Lights Revelation*, citing Tributsch, p. 216.

56 . Shallis, *The Electric Connection*, citing Leslie Hawkins, p. 41.

57 . Joan Price, *The Earth is Alive*, monograph (Denver, CO: Self-Published, 1981).

58 . Shallis, *The Electric Connection*, p. 176.

59 . Michael Norden, *Beyond Prozac* (New York: Regan Books, 1995).

60 . Becker, *Cross Currents*, p. 89.

61 . Shallis, *The Electric Connection*, p. 164.

62 . Shallis, *The Electric Connection*, p. 125.

63 . *Wired*, May 19, 1997.

64 . Lewis Thomas, *The Lives of a Cell* (New York: Viking Press, 1974), p. 74.

65 . Dr. Len Maler, University of Ottawa, "Electrosensory System of Weakly Electric Fish," at *http://aix1.uottawa.ca.*

66 . "Fish See with Electricity," *Denver Post*, June 15, 1997.

67 . Shallis, *The Electric Connection*, p. 248.

68 . Freeman Dyson, *Imagined Worlds* (Cambridge: Harvard University Press, 1997), pp. 134–135.

69 . Margaret Cheney, *Tesla: Man Out of Time* (New Jersey: Prentice Hall, 1981), p. 52.

70 . Cheney, *Tesla: Man Out of Time*, p. 55.

71 . Cheney, *Tesla: Man Out of Time*, p. 53.

72 . Cheney, *Tesla: Man Out of Time*, p. 74.

73 . Cheney, *Tesla: Man Out of Time*, p. 21.

74 . Wilhelm Reich, *The Function of the Orgasm* (New York: Farrar, Straus and Giroux, 1973).

75 . Itzhak Bentov, *Stalking the Wild Pendulum* (Rochester, VT: Destiny Books; distributed by Harper and Row, 1988), pp. 41—42.

76 . Bentov, *Stalking the Wild Pendulum*, p. 42.

77 . Jose Arguelles, *Earth Ascending* (Boulder, CO: Shambhala; distributed by Random House, 1984), p. 17.

78 . Norbert Wiener, *The Human Use of Human Beings* (New York: Doubleday and Archer, 1954), p. 26.

79 . Hans Moravec, "Pigs in Space," archived on Web site at *http://www.frc.ri.cmu.edu/~hpm/project.archive/general.articles/1992/CyberPigs.html*.

80 . Moravec, "Pigs in Space."

81 . Hans Moravec, *Mind Children* (Cambridge: Harvard University Press, 1988).

82 . Moravec, *Mind Children*, p. 68.

83 . Robert White, "The Mind-Brain Continuum: A Fifth Dimensional Concept," Conference on Brain Research and Human Consciousness, March 1986. Currently at *http://itest.slu.edu/dloads/80s/braincon.txt*.

84 . *Wired*, April 1998.

85 . Alexander Chislenko, "Networking in the Mind Age," 1996, archived on Web site at *http://www.ethologic.com/sasha/mindage.html*.

Chapter 5

1 . Peter Russell, *The Global Brain* (Los Angeles: Jeremy P. Tarcher, 1983).

2 . *http://www.saffo.com/infoworld_interview.html*

3 . Woodrow Wilson, "Final Address in Support of the League of Nations," delivered September 9, 1919, in Pueblo, Colorado.

4 . Hakim Bey, "Millenium" (Brooklyn: Autonomedia, and Dublin: Garden of Delights Publications, 1996), p. 17.

5 . Todd Gitlin, *Inside Prime Time* (New York: Pantheon, 1985), p. 332.

6 . William Irwin Thompson, *Imaginary Landscape* (New York: St. Martin's Press, 1989), p. 98.

7 . *Wall Street Journal, Interactive Edition*, September 28, 1998, *http://www.wsj.com*.

8 . Jack Valenti, Motion Picture Association of America, Press Release, June 8, 1999.

9 . Stewart Brand, *The Media Lab* (New York: Viking, 1986).

10 . The trend was satirized in the movie *Lost in Translation*.

11 . Bey, "Millenium."

12 . Bey, "Millenium."

13 . Bey, "Millenium."

14 . Ken Wilber, *A Brief History of Everything* (Boston: Shambhala, 2001).

15 . Francis Heylighen, "Why the Global Superorganism Must Evolve a Brain," Global Brain Workshop, 2002 at *http://pespmc1.vub.ac.be/Conf/GB-0.html.*

16 . Stanislav Grof, ed., *Human Survival and Consciousness Evolution* (Albany: SUNY Albany Press, 1980).

17 . Whittle also tried to turn education into a for-profit industry with the Edison Project, in partnership with former Yale University president Benno Schmitt.

18 . Jacques Valleé, *The Invisible College* (New York: E. P. Dutton, 1975), p. 198.

19 . Terence McKenna, *The Archaic Revival* (New York: HarperSanFrancisco, 1992), p. 72.

20 . It is worth noting that occult, or to be less judgmental, "transper-sonal" experiences are likely to occur at moments of extreme physical or emotional distress. Evidence of further psychic effects—telepathy or out-of-body experiences—seems strong only at the margins of human behavior and has never been replicated on a consistent enough basis to satisfy scientists (hence the term Margins of Reality). According to Grosso, "need and passion may sometimes cause our minds to separate from our bodies" (*The Final Choice*, p. 152).

21 . Michael Grosso, *The Final Choice* (Walpole, NH: Stillpoint Publishing, 1985), p. 199.

22 . Dennis Stillings, ed., *Cyberbiological Studies of the Imaginal Component in UFO Experiences* (Minneapolis: The Archaeus Project, 1985), p. 32.

23 . Jacques Valleé, *Messengers of Deception* (Berkeley, CA: And/Or Press, 1979), p. 85.

24 . Valleé, *Messengers of Deception*, p. 99.

25 . Valleé, *Confrontations* (New York: Random House, 1990), p. 90.

26 . Valleé, *Confrontations*, p. 188.

27 . Paul Devereux, *Earth Lights Revelation* (London: Blandford Press, 1989), p. 45.

28 . Devereux, *Earth Lights Revelation*, p. 201.

29 . Devereux, *Earth Lights Revelation*, p. 196.

30 . Devereux, *Earth Lights Revelation*, p. 178.

31 . Raymond Moody Jr., M.D., *Life After Life* (New York: Bantam, 1975).

32 . Kenneth Ring, *The Omega Project* (New York: Quill, 1992).

33 . Ring, *The Omega Project*, p. 11.

34 . Ring, *The Omega Project*, p. 144.

35 . Ring, *The Omega Project*, p. 156.

36 . Ring, *The Omega Project*, p. 156.

37 . Michael Grosso, in *The Final Choice*, attributes the term to Aldous Huxley.

38 . Grosso, *The Final Choice*, p. 63.

39 . Grosso, *The Final Choice*, p. 238.

40 . Grosso, *The Final Choice*, p. 223.

41 . Grosso, *The Final Choice*, p. 97.

42 . Grosso, *The Final Choice*, p. 75.

43 . Grosso, *The Final Choice*, p. 208.

44 . Grosso, *The Final Choice*, p. 210.

45 . Grosso, *The Final Choice*, pp. 205, 195.

46 . Grosso, *The Final Choice*, p. 239.

47 . Grosso, *The Millenium Myth*, p. 260.

48 . Grosso, *The Final Choice*, p. 155.

49 . Vernor Vinge, "Technological Singularity," *Whole Earth Review*, Winter, 1993.

50 . Vinge, "Technological Singularity."

51 . "Requiem for the Twentieth Century," *Magical Blend*, April 1995, p. 58.

52 . Dave Pape, "The Psychology of the Noosphere," published on *http://www.noogenesis.com*.

53 . Pesce, "Proximal and Distal Unity," published on *http://hyperreal.org/~mpesce/pdu.html*, May 25, 1996.

54 . Mark Pesce, "Proximal and Distal Unity." Incidentally, the developers characterized the lowest level or zone of the project as Code World. Twenty thousand lines of C code make up the piece. This is the wholistic substrate of the piece.

55 . Peter Russell, posting on Global Brain mailing list, Web site at *http://pespmc1.vub.ac.be/*.

56 . Jayne Gackenbush, Web site at *http://pespmc1.vub.ac.be/*.

57 . Mark Pesce, accessed June 1998 on Web site at *http://www.hyperreal.org/~mpesce/*.

58 . Mark Pesce, *http://www.xs4all.nl/~mpesce/*.

59 . Anthony Judge, "Information Highways to Songlines of the Noosphere," essay online at *http://www.laetusinpraesens.org/docs/songline.php*.

60 . Eric Raymond, "Homesteading the Noosphere," *First Monday*, April 1998 at *http://www.firstmonday.org/issues/issue3_10/raymond/index.html*.

61 . Raymond, "Homesteading the Noosphere."

62 . Judge, "Information Highways to Songlines of the Noosphere."

63 . Francis Heylighen and Johan Bollen, "The World Wide Web as a Super-Brain; From Metaphor to Model," archived on Web site at *http://pespmc1.vub.ac.be/papers/WWWSuperBRAIN.html.*

64 . This is reminiscent of Karl Pribram's holographic model of brain.

65 . Heylighen and Bollen, "The World Wide Web as a Super-Brain."

66 . Heylighen and Bollen, "The World Wide Web as a Super-Brain."

67 . Heylighen and Bollen, "The World Wide Web as a Super-Brain."

68 . Arthur Young, *The Reflexive Universe* (New York: Delacorte Press, 1976), p. 173.

69 . Ralph Abraham, Terence McKenna, and Rupert Sheldrake, *Trialogues at the Edge of the West* (Santa Fe: Bear and Co., 1992). pp. 50, 71.

70 . Teilhard de Chardin, *The Future of Man* (New York: Harper & Row, 1964), p. 311.

Afterword

1 . Francis Fukuyama, "History Is Still Going Our Way," *Wall Street Journal*, October 5, 2001.

Bibliography

Becker, Robert O. and Gary Selden. *The Body Electric*. New York: Morrow, 1985.

Dawkins, Richard. *The Selfish Gene*. Oxford: Oxford University Press, 1976, New York: 1978.

Devereux, Paul. *Earth Lights Revelation*. London: Blandford Press, 1989.

Evans, Hilary. *The SLI Effect*. London: ASSAP, 1993.

Goddard, Dwight, ed. *A Buddhist Bible*. Boston: Beacon Press, 1938, 1966.

Gregory, Richard L., ed. *The Oxford Companion to the Mind*. Oxford: Oxford University Press, 1987.

Grof, Christina. *The Thirst for Wholeness*. San Francisco: HarperSanFrancisco, 1993.

Grosso, Michael. *The Final Choice*. Walpole, NH: Stillpoint Publishing, 1985.

———. *The Millenium Myth*. Wheaton, IL: Quest Books, 1995.

Harman, Willis. *Global Mind Change*. New York: Warner Books, 1988.

Jung, Carl. *Archetypes and the Collective Unconscious*. Princeton: Bollingen, 1959, 1968.

Lilly, John. *The Center of the Cyclone*. New York: Julian Press, 1972.

Ludlow, Fitz Hugh. *The Hasheesh Eater*. New York: Harpers, 1857.

Lukas, Mary and Ellen Lukas. *Teilhard: A Biography*. New York: McGraw Hill, 1977.

McLuhan, Marshall. *Understanding Media: The Extensions of Man.*
New York: McGraw-Hill, 1964.

Moravec, Hans. *Mind Children.* Cambridge: Harvard University Press,
1988.

Murphy, Michael. *The Future of the Body.* New York: Jeremy P. Tarcher,
1992.

Neumann, Erich. *The Origins and History of Consciousness.* Princeton:
Bollingen, 1954.

Ornstein, Robert and Paul Ehrlich. *New World New Mind.* New York:
Doubleday, 1989.

Penfield, Wilder. *The Mystery of the Mind.* Princeton: Princeton University
Press, 1978.

Persinger, Michael. *Space-Time Transients and Unusual Events.* Chicago:
Nelson-Hall, 1977.

Ring, Kenneth. *The Omega Project.* New York: Quill, 1992.

Russell, Peter. *The Global Brain.* Los Angeles: Jeremy P. Tarcher, 1983.

Scholem, Gershom. *Kabbalah.* New York: Meridian, 1974, 1978.

Shallis, Michael. *The Electric Connection.* New York: New Amsterdam, 1988.

Sheldrake, Rupert. *New Science of Life: The Hypothesis of Formative Causation.*
New York: Jeremy P. Tarcher, 1981.

Stapledon, Olaf. *The Starmaker.* New York: Dover Publications, 1968.

Tart, Charles. *Transpersonal Psychologies.* New York: HarperCollins, 1983.

Teilhard de Chardin, Pierre. *The Phenomenon of Man.* New York:
Harper & Row, 1959.

———. *The Future of Man.* New York: Harper & Row, 1964.

Thomas, Lewis. The *Lives of a Cell: Notes of a Biology Watcher*. New York: Viking Press, 1974.

Thompson, William Irwin. *Imaginary Landscape: Making Worlds of Myth and Science*. New York: St. Martin's Press, 1989.

Thurman, Robert A. F., trans. *The Tibetan Book of the Dead: The Book of Liberation through Understanding of the Between*. New York: Bantam, 1994.

White, Frank. *The Overview Effect*. Boston: Houghton Mifflin, 1987.

Wilber, Ken. *The Atman Project*. Wheaton, IL: Quest Books, 1980.

Young, Arthur. *The Reflexive Universe: Evolution of Consciousness*. New York: Delacorte Press, 1976.

About the Author

Donald P. Dulchinos is currently Senior Vice President, Advanced Platforms and Services, for Cable Television Laboratories. He has been Director of Research, National Cable Television Association, Economic Analyst with National Economic Research Associates, and Technical Information Specialist at the United States Library of Congress. He holds a Master's Degree in Public Administration from the University of Denver Graduate School of Business and Public Management, and a B.A. in Economics from Union College in Schenectady, New York.

He is a charter member of the Board of Directors of the Boulder Community Network, a member of the Society of Satellite Professionals, Past President of the Kappa Alpha Literary Society, and a Conference Host on The Well. In 2005, he was winner of the second annual Award for Leadership in Interactive Television by *ITVT* (InteractiveTV Today) magazine and its panel of industry leaders.

He is the author of *Pioneer of Inner Space: The Life of Fitz Hugh Ludlow, Hasheesh Eater*, and *Forbidden Sacraments: The Survival of Shamanism in Western Civilization*.

For more information on the themes of this book, please visit *http://www.neurosphere.org*.

To Our Readers

Weiser Books, an imprint of Red Wheel/Weiser, publishes books across the entire spectrum of occult and esoteric subjects. Our mission is to publish quality books that will make a difference in people's lives without advocating any one particular path or field of study. We value the integrity, originality, and depth of knowledge of our authors.

Our readers are our most important resource, and we appreciate your input, suggestions, and ideas about what you would like to see published. Please feel free to contact us, to request our latest book catalog, or to be added to our mailing list.

Red Wheel/Weiser, LLC
P. O. Box 612
York Beach, ME 03910-0612
www.redwheelweiser.com